THE WINDOWSILL

HERB GARDEN

THE WINDOWSILL

HERB GARDEN

by

John Prenis

Elizabeth Corning Dudley, Editor

Alice Joy Carter, Consulting Editor, Food

RUNNING PRESS
PHILADELPHIA, PENNSYLVANIA

Canadian representatives: General Publishing Co., Ltd.,
30 Lesmill Road, Don Mills, Ontario M3B 2T6.
International representatives: Worldwide Media Services, Inc.,
115 East Twenty-third Street, New York, New York 10010.

9 8 7 6 5 4 3 2 1
The digit on the right indicates the number of this printing.

Library of Congress Cataloging-in-Publication Number 90–52739

ISBN 0–89471–890–8

Cover design by Toby Schmidt
Interior design by Stephanie Longo
Cover illustration by Kathy Lynn
Interior illustrations by Joan Poole
Typography by Commcor Communications, Philadelphia, PA
Printed and bound in the United States by Command Web Offset Company

This book may be ordered by mail from the publisher. Please add $2.50 for
postage and handling. *But try your bookstore first!*

Running Press Book Publishers
125 South Twenty-second Street
Philadelphia, Pennsylvania 19103

Recipes are reprinted and adapted from the following sources with the kind
permission of the publishers:

Fresh Herb Know-How by Frieda's Finest/Produce Specialties, Inc., © 1987:
Garlic-Herb Cheese Spread; Fresh Herb Vinaigrette; Quick Chicken
Scallopine; *Haricots Verts* Parisian Style; White Sauce Supreme; Mayonnaise
Vert; Fresh Herb Butter; and *Bouquet Garni*.

Recipes for a Kitchen Garden by Renee Shepherd, © 1987 by Shepherd's
Garden Publishing, Felton, CA: Green Bean Paté with Basil; Tomato, Opal
Basil, and Mozzarella Salad; Borage and Cucumbers in Sour Cream
Dressing; Basic Herbed Salad Dressing; Creamy Cress Salad Dressing;
Cheesy Chive Blossom Omelet; Thai Chicken with Basil; Butterflied Basil
Shrimp; Golden Brown Chive Roast Potatoes; Gorgonzola and Fresh Thyme
Sauce for Pasta; Homemade Dilled Mustard; *Salsa Fresca*; *Salsa de
Tomatillos*; Lemon Basil Marinade for Grilled Fish; Sorrel and Shallot
Butter; Herbed Flour; Herbal Salt Substitute; Scented Basil Vinegar; Chive
Blossom Vinegar; and Herbed Bread Sticks.

Shepherd's Garden Seeds Catalog, © 1990 by Shepherd's Garden Seeds,
Felton, CA: Linguini with Fresh Parsley Clam Sauce; and Roasted Potatoes
with Garlic and Herbs.

Cooking with Herbs by Susan Belsinger and Carolyn Dille, © 1984 by Van
Nostrand Reinhold, New York, NY: Eggplant Caviar; Goat Cheese Marinated
with Fresh Sage and Garlic; Black and White Bean Soup with Savory;
Grilled Lamb with Mustard-Tarragon Marinade; Fillet of Sole with Crab;
Butternut Purée with Thyme; Spiced Mushrooms; Bay Mustard Sauce;
Oregano Hot Sauce; Savory Peach Butter; Honeydew Chervil Sorbet;
Marjoram Corn Bread; Bay Rum Custard; and Mulled Rosemary Wine and
Black Tea.

Permission to reprint from *Farm Journal's Best-Ever Vegetable Recipes*,
© 1984, was granted by Farm Journal, Inc: Tomato-Dill Bisque; Cucumber
Refrigerator Pickles; Watercress and Nectarine Salad; Tabouli with Bean
Sprouts; Herbed Yogurt Dressing; Decidedly Dill Dressing; Green Goddess
Dressing; Creamy Cucumber-Dill Dressing; Béarnaise Sauce; Pesto; Aioli
Sauce; Sour Cream-Dill Topping; Mixed Herb Butter; Lemon-Parsley Butter;
and Dill Butter.

Recipes courtesy of The American Spice Trade Association: Low-Sodium
French Seasoning Blend; Herb Blend; Herb Seasoning Blend; and
Blackened Seasoning Blend.

Table of Contents

Growing Herbs

*H*erbs are a delight, pleasing our senses of smell and taste, bringing color and freshness to every place where they flourish. They can add new interest to ordinary dishes and complement the most exotic foods. With a pinch of herbs, routine food preparation becomes creative cookery, and an everyday meal an adventure. There is nothing like the fun of gardening combined with the pleasure of flavoring a meal with an herb you have grown yourself.

Herbs are the ideal project for a beginning gardener. They are not fussy about soil, they resist pests, and they can be grown almost anywhere in North America with a minimum of care. A windowsill box, several pots, or small patch of ground in your yard will provide you with a plentiful supply of herbs for your kitchen. All you have to do is pinch off a few aromatic leaves whenever you need them to flavor a favorite dish. At the end of the growing season you can harvest the plants and dry their leaves or gather their seeds for future use.

In general, an herb is any plant valued for its scent, its use in flavoring foods, or its medicinal use. This definition includes such diverse plants as willow trees (whose bark contains salicin, the precursor to aspirin) and catnip (whose scent is certainly a pleasure to your cat). In this book we are interested in the plants commonly known as culinary herbs, whose leaves and seeds are used to flavor foods. In contrast to spices, which are usually tropical, most culinary herbs grow well in temperate zones, and thrive over most of North America.

Many people wonder, "What is the correct way to pronounce the word 'herb'?" In any gathering of gardeners or chefs it becomes evident very quickly that some people say "herb" and others say "erb." Opinion seems to be about equally divided as to which is the better choice. Dictionaries list both pronunciations as correct, so it seems to be a matter of individual preference. My recommendation is to please yourself. Whichever you choose, you'll be in good company.

The discovery and first uses of herbs are unknown. It seems likely that discovery came about by accident, perhaps when someone walking through the brush was arrested by the pungent odor of a plant. It may have seemed like magic when herbs were first used with food—that such a tiny bit of leaves could cause such wonderful changes in flavors. Herbs must have seemed to have special powers, and it is no wonder that they quickly became tangled in myth, magic, and ritual.

The written record of their use extends back at least to the time when the pyramids of Egypt were being built, more than 4,000 years ago. Early civilizations (China, India, Egypt) used herbs to flavor foods, but their role in medicine was paramount. This emphasis continued until advances in the laboratory made it possible to synthesize many medicines.

A particularly interesting early use of herbs was as perfumes, deodorants, and fumigants—a reflection of the pervasive unsavory odors of bygone days. In the time of Charlemagne, for example, the cold stone floors of monasteries and castles were strewn with fragrant herbs (known as strewing herbs), and gentlemen carried herbal nosegays to clear their nostrils of the unpleasant odors they encountered all too often.

During the Dark Ages of Europe, manuscripts of early herbal lore were preserved and copied by hand in medieval monasteries. There, herbs were grown in enclosed gardens and were valued for their medicinal and religious significance. With the Renaissance came increased trade between cultures and the invention of printing. Many old collections of herbal lore became widely available, and new ones were written.

Herbals often mixed accurate descriptions of plants with fantasy and folklore. Each herb was assigned a place in the zodiac; e.g., basil with Scorpio, bay with Leo. Medicines were frequently determined by the Doctrine of Signatures, which held that every plant had been given signs by which its curative virtues could be identified. A plant that attracted bees, for instance, was thought to be good for bee stings. Extensive collections of remedies were built up, and many are still of interest and value. The word *officinalis* or *officinale* in an herb's Latin name indicates that it once had a medicinal use.

When the colonization of the New World began, herbs accompanied the first immigrants. Unable to rely on their distant homeland, European settlers fell back on familiar remedies and flavorings. Many native plants used by the Indians proved helpful, and were adopted by the settlers. Every homestead had an herb garden, and carefully packed herb seeds were carried westward.

Twentieth-century transportation has made spices readily available. With improved sanitation, and drugstores stocked with manufactured medicines and artificial deodorants, the need for herbs seems to have declined. Yet botanists still explore the world's rain forests, learning about the curative powers of exotic plants from native peoples; Chinese herb-gatherers roam remote hills and forests in search of medicinal plants; gardeners everywhere are rediscovering the pleasure of growing sweet-scented, flavorful herbs; professional chefs garnish their creations with ever more exotic greenery; and students thrive on oregano-studded pizza. Herbs are in their ascendancy once again. As you grow and use some of the plants described in this book, you will become part of a community of happy enthusiasts. Welcome!

Growing Herbs Indoors

Your indoor herb garden can be one of the most cheerful and beautiful parts of your home. Whether you devote an entire room to your herbs or just a windowsill, their unique fragrances, colors, and flavors will stimulate your senses and spark your imagination. The little care they require will reward you many times over.

You can easily grow herbs indoors if you keep in mind that they are basically outdoor plants. Herbs prefer temperatures below 70° F, so many homes are too hot, dry, and stuffy for them, especially in wintertime. Never place plants on a radiator or near a hot air vent. You can provide extra humidity by leaving pans of water near your plants, or by putting their pots in a tray filled with pebbles, then filling the tray with water to just below the top of the pebbles. The higher humidity is good for you, too!

The answer to the question of how much light you need to raise herbs is simple—all you can get! Give your herbs a window that gets as much sun as possible. Two or three hours of sun a day is enough for several herbs, and some herbs thrive in a window that gets light, but not direct sun. Herbs grown primarily for their seed should not be grown indoors because they might not get enough light to flower and set seed. You can supplement natural light with artificial light to ensure maximum healthy growth. One way is to place a fluorescent lamp about 15 to 20 inches above your plants and give them about 15 hours of light a day.

Water is important, too. Most herbs should be watered whenever the surface of the soil feels dry. Check all of your plants every day, but only water ones that need it. It's a good idea to keep your watering-can full so the water will be at room temperature. If you do use water straight from the tap, make sure it is tepid. Give your plants a fine spray of water (misting) every day or two if you can; it helps wash dust from their leaves and provides healthy humidity.

Good drainage is essential to grow herbs successfully. All of the herbs in this book, with the exception of the mints, require well-drained soil. They simply will not prosper with water standing around their roots. Pots should, and usually do, have drainage holes in them to let excess water run out into a holder beneath the pot. Indoor windowboxes usually come with holders. Before putting in any soil, fill the bottom quarter of each pot with pebbles or pieces of old broken pots to ensure good drainage away from the roots.

Herbs are not fussy about soil. Nearly any soil that will grow weeds will grow herbs. Most herbs can survive in dry, rocky soil much poorer than anything you will give them. However, preparing your soil carefully will bring big dividends. Herbs generally grow best in soil to which a lot of organic compost has been added, and that has been turned over thoroughly with a fork or spade. In most cases the soil should be slightly acid to neutral. For plants that prefer an alkaline soil, add some crushed eggshells, a little lime, or bone meal.

The nutrients in a pot of soil or windowbox are limited, depleted by the demands of the plant and the constant passage of water through the soil. For this reason, many

The Windowsill Herb Garden

growers recommend that you feed your indoor plants every couple of weeks with a liquid fertilizer. Make sure to follow instructions. Do not overfertilize; too much fertilizer is far more likely to kill a plant than too little.

Always start with good soil that has a fair amount of organic matter in it to provide nutrients and minerals. A simple soil mixture for herbs consists of equal parts of soil, sand, and humus. The humus can be peat moss, aged compost, or rotted leaves. If you have just one windowbox or a few pots of herbs, you might want to buy a bag of prepared soil from a local nursery.

Herbs are not very likely to be bothered by insect pests. Herbs are full of aromatic oils that appeal to us but repel many insects. Healthy herbs usually shrug off the attacks of pests outdoors, but the less-than-ideal conditions indoors may weaken them to the point that they become vulnerable. The best preventative is to wash the entire plant, including the undersides of leaves, under the tap each week. This removes both insects and their eggs. If an infestation does develop, a stronger treatment is to wash the plant with a quart of water to which a little detergent has been added. Be sure to rinse the plant very thoroughly. If your best efforts fail to get rid of an insect pest, it is better for your health to throw the plant away than to resort to sprays.

There is not much more you need do for your indoor plants. Turn them from time to time to keep them symmetrical, pick off dead leaves, and trim back scraggly growth to keep them looking neat. With just a little attention each day, your indoor herb garden will be a source of constant enjoyment.

Growing Herbs from Seed

Most herbs are easy to grow from seed. This is by far the least expensive and most exciting method and is most useful for small indoor herb gardens. Not every herb is best grown from seed, however. Beginners should buy slow-growing herbs, such as rosemary, as plants from nurseries. Some herbs, such as tarragon, cannot be grown from seed at all.

Starting herbs from seed indoors has the advantage of giving your plants a head start if you have a short growing season. Seeds can be started in the soil mix described earlier for growing herbs indoors. Keep the seedbed (a plant flat, some pots, or a container with peat pellets) in dim light until the seeds sprout, and then place it in full light. Your seeds will sprout faster if you put their seedbed in a warm place.

Plant your seed to the depth recommended on the seed packets. If you don't have this information, a useful rule of thumb is to plant the seeds to two or three times their width. Very fine seed can just be sprinkled on the soil. When you are done, firm the soil to ensure good contact between soil and seed.

The germination times given in this book are only a rough guide as to when your seeds will sprout. The actual times vary quite a bit, depending mainly on soil temperature. An unseasonable cold spell could set your seeds back a few days, or a warm spell could speed them up.

You may have trouble with "damping off" when starting plants indoors. This is a fungus which rots the seedlings' roots. It is aggravated by too much warmth, dampness, or poor air circulation. Once it strikes, there is little you can do except start over. Commercially sold seed-starting soil mixtures are sterilized to kill this fungus—you may want to invest in a bag or two. You can also sterilize your own soil by baking it for two hours in a 300° F oven.

Once your seeds have sprouted, water the seedlings gently with a fine spray to keep the soil from drying out, and to avoid washing them out of the soil, whenever necessary. You may want to shield your young plants from the sun at first if the days are hot and bright.

The first two leaves a young seedling holds up to the light are the "seed leaves" which were once inside the seed. They are smoothly rounded and usually do not resemble the true leaves which appear later. True leaves look like the leaves of an adult plant.

There are usually more seeds in a packet than you can use, so when your seedlings are two or three inches tall, it's time to "thin them out," or pull up the extra plants. This is a painful task, but it must be done to give your remaining plants room to grow.

Seedlings with two to four true leaves are ready to be transplanted into small pots, an operation gardeners call "pricking off." Use a pencil to poke a shallow hole in the soil where the seedling is to be planted. (By the way, that pencil has now become a "dibble.") Lift each young plant gently out of its seed bed with a blunt, flat instrument such as a spoon handle or tongue depressor, taking care to disturb the roots as little as possible. Then place the seedling in the hole and carefully firm the soil around its roots.

Peat pellets make starting seeds as easy as possible. You don't need to prick off individual seedlings started in a peat pellet—the entire pellet can (and should) be planted in your garden.

Growing Herbs from Cuttings

Some of the herbs in this book should be started from cuttings rather than seeds. A cutting is a section taken from a mature plant and placed in soil until it develops roots of its own. This is not difficult, and it can be rewarding.

Take cuttings in the spring if you want the plants for that year, or in late summer if you want them for the winter. Find a mature but not woody section on the plant from which you are taking cuttings; it should still bend quite easily. Cut several pieces three to four inches long. Strip the leaves from the lower third of the cuttings, and place their stems in a moist medium (a good one is equal parts of potting soil, fine sand, and peat moss). Put several cuttings in the same pot, and water them gently but thoroughly. Cover the pot with a plastic bag, and use small sticks around the edges of the pot to hold the bag away from the cuttings. Place the pot in the light, but not in direct sunlight.

Spray your cuttings each day to maintain humidity. When their tops start to put out new growth it means that they are taking root. This usually takes two to three weeks for herbs. At this point you can remove the plastic. Water your cuttings for a few more days, and then transplant them to their permanent homes.

Growing Herbs Outdoors

Many people, when thinking of herb gardens, picture the elaborately patterned, traditional sort found in botanical gardens and on large estates. You need plan nothing so complicated. A one-foot long outdoor windowbox provides enough space for one plant of each of four different kinds of herbs. You can also grow a fine selection in a few flower pots placed in the sun. Four or five plants of each kind will yield all the herbs you can use, unless you want more to dry or freeze for the winter.

In your garden, you will probably have both annuals and perennials. Annuals, as the name implies, last only one season. Perennials, on the other hand, have roots that survive the winter, even though the above-ground parts may look dead after the growing season.

If planting a garden in your yard, any convenient patch of ground will do, but a spot near the kitchen door has obvious advantages. Place your plants so that you can easily reach all parts of your garden without stepping on anything. It's a good idea to put tall plants in the back so they won't shade shorter ones. A nice layout is a pie-shaped bed, with different kinds of herbs filling up each of the "slices."

Outdoors, poor drainage can be avoided by using containers with drainage holes such as windowboxes, pots, or barrel halves. If you plant in your yard, avoid low-lying spots that collect water every time it rains. Soil that is heavy with clay drains poorly and should be mixed with sand until water drains away freely. Wet soil can also be avoided by making a "sandbox-style" raised bed with railroad ties to enclose good soil to a depth of about six inches.

If you plan to put young plants outdoors which you have started indoors, they must first go through a process of acclimation known as "hardening off." This involves gradually exposing them to outdoor conditions while protecting them from full sun and strong winds. At the end of two weeks they should be ready to be planted in your garden.

Seed can be sown outdoors as soon as the soil warms in the spring. Clear the place you have chosen, loosen the soil thoroughly, add compost if it is a new spot, and then smooth the soil and soak it thoroughly before planting the seeds. The seeds of some hardy plants can be sown in the fall, after Indian summer, and covered with a layer of mulch. The cold keeps them dormant, while snow and frost soften seed coats. When the soil warms in the spring, the little plants are ready to go.

Some perennial herbs are grown outdoors as annuals because they are killed by cold winters. However, they are perennial when given the chance. If you are in doubt about an herb surviving the winters in your area, check with a local nursery or a fellow grower. To help outdoor perennials survive the winter, it's a good idea to cover them with mulch. A couple of inches of dead leaves, straw or hay, pine needles, old Christmas tree branches, or bark chips are all excellent mulches. The idea is to insulate the bed and prevent the alternate freezing and thawing so destructive to roots. Remove the mulch once spring has arrived to stay. Underneath you will find your herbs already putting out new shoots, as well as new seedlings from seeds that were dropped the previous fall.

Twenty-five Useful Herbs

*E*very herb has its own rich and fascinating history. Herb gardens were the medicine chests of ancient physicians, and many herbs are still used medicinally. Through the centuries, they have symbolized strength, fertility, accomplishment, happiness, and other qualities. They have been considered omens of good or evil, and often have been attributed magical powers.

You can find common and exotic herbs to suit almost any garden, but some varieties have special needs. One may require a great deal of direct sunlight, while another may prefer shade. Some grow well from seed and transplant easily, but others do not. Some species may be harvested as seedlings, and others only when mature.

Understanding your herbs' needs will help you keep them looking and tasting their best, and knowing their histories will increase your appreciation of these beautiful—and useful—plants.

Basil *Ocimum basilicum*

—MINT FAMILY—

Basil has a fascinating history. Native to India, it is sacred to the Hindus; holy basil (*Ocimum sanctum*) is planted around homes and temples to purify the air and ward off evil. A leaf placed on the breast of a dead person is believed to provide an entrance to Paradise.

The ancient Greeks considered basil an antidote to the basilisk, a mythical serpent whose breath and glance were said to be fatal. They also believed that the planting of basil should be accompanied by cursing, a custom still followed by some growers. To the Italians, basil was a sign of love, and even now a sprig of basil is sometimes worn as a love charm.

Basil is a handsome herb that can grow to a height of two and a half to three feet. It has bright, shiny, green, oval leaves about two inches long, small white flowers that usually start blooming in July, and a sweet, aromatic odor. A number of varieties are useful in cooking. The purple-leaved *Ocimum basilicum* 'Purpurascens' makes a strikingly colored and delicious vinegar. Some basils have intriguing flavors, such as *O. americanum* 'lemon,' *O. basilicum* 'cinnamon,' and *O. basilicum* 'anise.'

Basil thrives in well-drained, humus-rich soil, in full sun or partial shade. It is very easy to grow from seed and germinates in less than a week in warm soil. Young plants transplant easily, and should be placed in warm soil about a foot apart.

Basil does nicely indoors if kept pinched back and not allowed to flower—since it is an annual, it soon dies if allowed to flower and go to seed. Pinching off the tips of the branches also keeps the plant compact and bushy, and gives you a steady supply of leaves for cooking. Keep the soil barely moist and feed with liquid fertilizer about once a month. Basil must be grown from seed each year, but if your plants like the conditions you have given them, they will spread their own seed freely.

Sow basil outdoors once the soil has warmed in the spring; it does not germinate well in cold ground.

Basil has a strong flavor that becomes stronger with cooking. Its chief fame is that it combines well with tomatoes in any form. It is also useful in meats, seafood, cheese and egg dishes, poultry, soups, stews, and sauces.

Bay *Laurus nobilis*

—LAUREL FAMILY—

Bay leaves come from the laurel tree, a small, handsome evergreen with a noble place in myth and history.

The Greeks called bay "the Daphne tree" after the mythical nymph who turned into a laurel to escape the advances of Apollo. Apollo then pronounced the tree sacred. Through time laurel became a symbol of victory, joy, and triumph. Wreaths of laurel crowned Greek kings and heroes. From the words for laurel berry (*bacca lauri*) come the words baccalaureate and bachelor, both indications of academic success and achievement. In ancient Rome, scrolls proclaiming victory were bound with laurel. It was also believed that laurel trees purified the air, and when epidemics came, Roman emperors moved to the country where laurel trees grew.

Early herbalists recorded that bay leaves were soothing when added to the bath, gave strength when brewed in a potion, and kept one sober when tucked behind the ear.

Some even said that neither witch or devil, nor thunder or lightning, could harm a man near a bay tree. Be that as it may, bay leaves were used to ornament churches well into the last century, especially at Christmastime.

Since bay is notoriously difficult to grow from seed, and since cuttings can take many months to root, it is probably most satisfactory to start with a young plant from a local nursery. While the laurel is a small tree, it is still a tree. It is also a subtropical plant and cannot withstand freezing. It is best grown outdoors in a tub and wintered indoors in a cool, partially shaded place protected from direct sunlight.

Residents of warmer states can grow laurel trees outdoors. Choose a sheltered location, provide rich soil, keep your plant well watered, and be prepared to protect it from frost—a threat not uncommon even as far south as Miami.

A single bay leaf gives a fine flavor to a soup or a stew, and enhances almost all meat, poultry, or fish dishes. Try bay also in sauces, salad dressings, and stuffings.

Borage   Borago officinalis

—BORAGE FAMILY—

Borage is an interesting herb. It has been given the common names bee-bread, starflower, and herb-of-gladness. The first refers to its attractiveness to bees, for whom it is often grown; the second to its attractive, star-shaped, azure-blue flowers; and the third to its cheering and stimulating qualities. The name *officinalis* was bestowed upon it for this last reason. The Greeks and Romans drank borage in wine to drive away sorrow and bring courage, and a stirrup cup with borage leaves floating in it was given to crusaders leaving for war. Modern research indicates that borage contains chemicals that affect the adrenal gland, which releases adrenalin at times of crisis.

Borage is a sprawling annual with lush and very hairy leaves. More than anything else, it resembles a monster African violet, if you can imagine an African violet two feet tall. Its star-shaped flowers appear in July if the seed is sown in March, and continue through the summer. Borage flowers have striking black centers. Their petals are pink when they first open, and later become blue.

Borage is easy to grow from seed and requires little care. Give it rich soil and plenty of sun. The seeds should be sown in their permanent locations, since borage does not transplant well. Germination time is about 10 days.

Indoors, give borage rich soil, a cool spot, plenty of sun, and a good-sized pot to accommodate its rather long taproot. Water it often enough to keep it moist. Trim it back from time to time to keep it about a foot high and moderately compact—unless you plan to startle your friends by placing it among your African violets!

Outdoors, seedlings should be thinned to about a foot apart. Mature plants self-sow freely in the fall, ensuring a new crop the following year. Do not restrict borage to your herb garden. When grown among other plants it is said to increase their resistance to pests and disease; it is a particularly good companion plant for strawberries.

Borage leaves have a pleasant cucumber flavor. Try them in salads or pickle them. It is best to use young leaves, since they are less hairy. Unfortunately they do not dry well, but fresh leaves are good to float in cool drinks. Iced borage tea is a refreshing summer drink.

Catnip Nepeta cataria

—MINT FAMILY—

Catnip is an herb that you are far more likely to find in a pet shop than at a spice counter. This was not always so, for in the fifteenth century catnip was used to season soups and stews. Legend has it that chewing its roots makes one quarrelsome, which is strange when you consider that catnip tea is known for its soothing effect. In addition to being enjoyed as a pleasing beverage, catnip tea was once used to relieve colds, fever, hysteria, headaches, and nightmares. It was also popular in Europe before the introduction of Chinese tea.

Catnip was brought to the New World by the Pilgrims, who introduced it to the Indians. The Indians took to it at once. It's nice to think that, after learning about so many new plants from the Indians, the settlers were able to return the favor.

Today, catnip is principally used as a treat for cats, who often become excited by its fragrance and dash about wildly. This may be its oldest use as well, for the Greeks and Romans knew of catnip and grew it for their pets.

Catnip is a rather untidy-looking perennial that grows to about three feet in height. Its heart-shaped, scalloped leaves are covered with velvety down. Pink flowers appear from July through September.

Catnip does well in dry, sandy soil and bright sun. It is extremely hardy and can survive droughts and frigid winters. It is sometimes found growing wild near old farmhouses.

Catnip is easily grown from seed, which can be sown either in spring or late fall and germinates in about 10 days. As long as your young plants are not disturbed, they are not likely to be bothered by cats. However, if a leaf is bruised or broken you will soon find every cat in the neighborhood rolling in your catnip bed. Fortunately, as the plants get older their stems grow woody, and they become far less vulnerable to this sort of damage.

Catnip tea not only soothes and aids digestion, but also contains healthy amounts of vitamins A and C. To make it, simply pour a cup of boiling water over a teaspoon of the dried, crumbled leaves and allow it to steep for a few minutes.

Chervil Anthriscus cerefolium

—CARROT FAMILY—

Chervil was a favorite of both the Greeks and Romans, who cooked the leaves like spinach and ate the roots as vegetables. The Roman historian Pliny recommended it as a warming dish for cold stomachs, and vinegar in which its seeds had been soaked as a cure for hiccups. During the Middle Ages, chervil was said to be wholesome and charming to the spirits. It was supposed to purify the blood in the spring, and its dried leaves were used to relieve bruises and painful joints. The roots were eaten to ward off the plague. Because of its reputed rejuvenating qualities, chervil came to symbolize resurrection and new life. To this day, chervil soup is eaten on Holy Thursday in parts of Europe.

Chervil is an annual that grows to a height of two feet. It has light green, fernlike, almost lacy leaves that resemble parsley but have the delicate flavor of licorice. As the leaves mature they become pink-red and rather tough. The blossoms are small and white, grouped in clusters, and followed by long, thin, black seeds.

Chervil is a grand indoor plant, easily started from seed and grown in pots. Like its relative, parsley, it needs well-drained, moderately rich, light soil. An added advantage is that it does not need full sunlight—in fact, it prefers coolness and shade. The only disadvantage to growing chervil indoors is that you may not have enough space to grow as much as you want!

You should sow chervil in its permanent location, since its delicate root system does not transplant well. Sprinkle the seed on top of the soil, scratch it lightly, and then gently press it down. Germination time is about two weeks, and fast-growing plants mature in about six weeks. Thin the seedlings to eight inches apart. About three square feet of garden space should hold all the chervil you need.

Young leaves are best for cooking, so it is a good idea to make several plantings a couple of weeks apart to ensure a continuous supply. Because the leaves are so fine, you will also want to have a number of plants growing at a time. It is important to water your plants well, or they may flower and set seed before you can gather their tender leaves. Pick leaves from the outside of the plant to give the center a chance to grow.

The flavor that chervil leaves give to food is like that of parsley, but more subtle; it has been called the gourmet's parsley. It blends so well with other herbs that it is almost never found alone. It is a vital ingredient of *fines herbes*, the mixture of chopped herbs used in many French dishes. Because of its amiable nature, it can be used freely almost anywhere.

Chives Allium schoenoprasum
—LILY FAMILY—

Chives have a long history. They were known 2,000 years ago to the Chinese, who used them to control bleeding and as an antidote to poisons, and also to the Egyptians and the ancient Greeks. They were planted extensively in the herb gardens of the Middle Ages, and later were brought by colonists to America.

Chives look almost exactly like the wild onions that are so hard to eradicate from lawns. Their thin blades grow to a foot in height from a mass of tiny underground bulbs. The flower is a soft purple ball that appears in early June and is pretty enough to earn this plant a place in any garden border.

Chives are perennial, hardy even in cold climates. They can be started from seed, but germination is slow and requires a combination of darkness, moisture, and temperatures from 60° to 70° F. Since this is a plant that divides easily and benefits from being divided, you might prefer to get a clump from a fellow gardener.

Chives are very easy to grow indoors, and do particularly well in windowsill containers, as they need plenty of sun. Feed them every couple of weeks with a liquid fertilizer, especially if you cut them frequently, and make sure they have plenty of moisture. If they seem to be doing poorly they may just need dividing or repotting.

Outdoors, plant clumps of four to six bulbs about six inches apart in sandy loam soil in full sun. After a couple of years, you should pull apart your clumps into several smaller ones to replant or share with other enthusiasts. This prevents overcrowding.

To harvest your chives, simply cut a few blades from near the base of the clump and snip them into small bits.

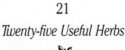

21

This is a strong grower and will send up new shoots quickly.

The method for drying other herbs does not work well for chives. To dry chives, spread a thin layer of non-iodized salt on a cookie sheet. Spread your chives over the salt, and cover them with another thin layer of salt. Place them in a 200° F oven 10 to 15 minutes. When done, sift the dried chives from the salt and crumble them into jars. Save the salt, too—it is now chive salt, and can be used in the same way you use onion or garlic salt.

Chives have a delicate onion flavor that goes well with soups, fish, eggs, bread, meats, vegetables, salads, and cheese dishes.

Allium tuberosum, known as Chinese or garlic chives, is another popular species with a somewhat stronger flavor and lovely clusters of starlike white flowers that bloom toward the end of summer.

Coriander (Cilantro) Coriandrum sativum
—CARROT FAMILY—

Like many herbs, coriander has a long history in many parts of the world. The Chinese used it to confer immortality. Seeds have been discovered in ancient Egyptian tombs, and coriander is one of the bitter herbs of Passover. In a very different vein, it is mentioned in *The Thousand and One Nights of Arabia*, and was an ingredient of love potions during the Middle Ages and Renaissance. This versatile plant came with the colonists to North America, and it is now widely naturalized here.

When a recipe calls for cilantro, it refers to the leaves of this plant. The more traditional name of coriander refers to the seeds. Of all the herbs described in this book, this is the only one you may not want to bring indoors. The mature plant and its unripe seeds have a decidedly unpleasant, rather buggy odor. (The name coriander is derived from the Greek for bedbug, a reference to this odor.) By contrast, the ripened and thoroughly dried seeds have a pleasant spicy aroma that only improves over time.

Coriander is an annual that grows to about three feet in height. It does well in a sunny location in light, rich, moist soil with good drainage. Because it germinates slowly and needs a full growing season to reach maturity, plant it as soon as the danger of frost is over in your area. Like other members of the carrot family, it does not transplant well and should be planted in its permanent location. Thin seedlings to at least four inches apart. Do not fertilize it during the growing season; this might actually make it less flavorful.

Coriander tastes rather like sage with lemon overtones. The fresh young leaves are the most flavorful and may be picked at any time. Seeds can be harvested by late summer. To do this, pick the whole plants and hang them in a dry place for several days over paper to catch the seeds that fall. Shake out the others, and store your crop in tightly closed jars.

Coriander is used in spicing, curries, and sausages. The leaves are a nice addition to stews and pilafs.

Dill Arethum graveolens
—CARROT FAMILY—

Dill has been known for thousands of years and has been used in many ways. It is mentioned in an Egyptian medical papyrus from 3,000 B.C. Its taste is said to stimulate the appetite and digestion, and its smell to arouse the brain, fire the will, and overcome the depressing effects of fatigue and stale air. It was burned as incense by the Greeks and Romans, and wreaths of dill were hung to freshen the air of kitchens and banquet halls.

The name "dill," from the Norse *dilla*, "to lull," indicates its use as a sedative, particularly for babies. Apparently it was thought to have a soothing effect on the upper atmosphere as well, for it was burned to drive away thunderstorms. It may have been equally effective against witches. Part of a seventeenth-century poem reads:

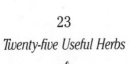

There with her Vervain and her Dill
That hindreth witches of their will.

One more use: brides used to put dill in their shoes, along with a sprinkling of salt, for good luck.

Dill is an upright, branching plant with blue-green, feathery foliage that resembles fennel. The flowers are yellow and lacy, somewhat like Queen Anne's Lace.

Dill is very easy to grow from seed and is a hardy annual. Germination time is about a week and a half, and the young plants mature in about six weeks. Growing dill indoors is not difficult, but it requires plenty of light— at least four hours of direct sunlight daily. A south-facing window is ideal. Keep the plants slightly moist. Dill grows about a foot tall indoors.

Once dill blooms it is practically all stem and flower, so if you are growing it for its leaves you should make several plantings a few weeks apart. When the flowers are mature, cut the flowering stems and hang them in bunches in a dark, dry spot over paper. When dry, the seeds will fall to the paper for you to collect and use.

You can plant dill outdoors in the spring after any danger of frost has passed. Like many plants with long taproots, dill does not transplant well and should be started in its permanent location. Outdoors, it can grow to three feet or more in height, so plant it behind shorter plants in your garden. Give it plenty of sun and well-drained, fertilized soil. When seedlings are two inches tall, thin them to about six inches apart. You can bring in outdoor plants and keep them through the winter.

The entire dill plant is aromatic, so the stalks, leaves, flowers, and seeds can be used in cooking. The seeds are seeds and everything else is "weed." The seeds have the stronger flavor, and are good in bread, bean soup, and, of course, pickles. Dill weed is good for flavoring fish, potatoes, peas, salads, sauces, meats, and vinegar.

Fennel *Foeniculum vulgare*

—CARROT FAMILY—

It is said that the early Greeks named fennel after the city of Marathon, where they achieved a great victory over the Persians. Another theory is that its early name was *marathron*, derived from a word that meant "to grow thin." Fennel has certainly enjoyed a reputation of helping people grow thin, and is still sometimes recommended to dieters. Medieval churchgoers nibbled on its seeds to keep them from getting too hungry during long services.

Fennel was also used to treat eye ailments, and Pliny believed snakes ate it after shedding their skins to help regain their eyesight. Like many herbs, during medieval times fennel was considered effective against witchcraft. It was often hung over doorways to keep out evil spirits.

Fennel is a perennial herb related to dill and coriander. It has feathery leaves and flat-topped clusters of bright yellow flowers. Both leaves and seeds are used in cooking. It's best not to place fennel close to dill; these plants can hybridize and the resulting seeds may not retain their characteristic flavors. Likewise, placing it too close to coriander may prevent the seeds of both herbs from forming at all.

Like dill, fennel can be grown indoors as a container plant. It needs at least four hours of direct sunlight each day. Keep the soil slightly moist, and trim the plants so they don't get too tall.

Plant fennel in well-drained, rich soil in a sunny location. Since it can grow up to five feet in height outdoors, plant it toward the back of your garden. Make especially sure that the bed is well watered until the first leaves develop.

You can begin to harvest your plants and use them throughout the growing season once they have put out a number of leaves. Harvest the seeds just as they begin to turn from green to brown; once ripe, they fall very quickly. Cut off the entire flowering heads, put them in a paper bag, and keep them in a warm, dry place until completely dried.

Often called the "fish herb," fennel goes quite well with any fish recipe. Add fresh leaves to the water when poaching fish, and use them as an ingredient in fish sauces. Fennel leaves counteract the heaviness of oily fish particularly well. The seeds add an agreeable anise flavor to breads and pastries, and are often used in sweet pickles.

25

Twenty-five Useful Herbs

Garden Cress   *Lepidium sativum*

—MUSTARD FAMILY—

This peppery-tasting relative of mustard is a good source of vitamin C, and was once used to prevent scurvy and cleanse the blood. It is believed to be native to western Asia or northern Africa, but it escaped from gardens and now grows wild in many parts of Europe and North America.

Cress is grown primarily as a salad plant, but the roots are sometimes used as a condiment. In Abyssinia the seeds are pressed to obtain an edible mustard-flavored oil.

Cress is an annual and a rapid grower—some of its closest relatives are troublesome weeds. Although it can grow to about 16 inches in height, it is usually eaten in the seedling stage. If left alone it puts forth small white flowers in early summer, followed by oval seed pods.

Cress is a particularly fine indoor plant. It doesn't even need soil! Simply sprinkle the seeds on anything soft and absorbent, such as a pan lined with paper towels. Soak the seeds thoroughly and cover them with wax paper for two days. When they have sprouted, remove the wax paper and place the pan in a window. Since garden cress does not need bright sunlight, even a north window is fine. Keep the seedlings moist until they are tall enough to use (about two inches). By planting new batches of seeds every two weeks you can have fresh young cress all winter long.

To grow cress outdoors, sprinkle the seeds over the ground and cover them lightly with fine soil. To keep the bed moist, gently water it each day with a fine spray until the cress is about two inches tall, ready to cut and use. This will be in about two weeks.

The smell and peppery taste of garden cress leave no doubt that it is a member of the mustard family. In fact, one of its wild relatives is known as "peppergrass." The tangy sprouts are excellent in salads and sandwiches, and make an attractive garnish.

Garlic *Allium sativum*

—LILY FAMILY—

The recorded use of garlic goes back at least 4,000 years, when it was known to both the Egyptians and the Chinese for its medicinal properties. The Chinese considered it effective in the treatment of high blood pressure. It achieved particular prominence in Egypt, where its reputation for building strength and endurance made it a staple food for slaves engaged in the formidable task of building the Pyramids. The Romans considered garlic the herb of Mars, the god of war, and ate it for strength in battle.

Garlic was also believed to have powers against evil. In many countries, cloves of garlic were worn around children's necks to protect them from evil spirits, and garlic is also a well-known charm against vampires.

This perennial relative of chives and onions has a bulb that is made up of 10 to 15 bulblets, or cloves. Garlic grows to about two feet in height as a clump of long, slender leaves arising from the bulb. Pink to whitish flowers appear in late summer in a head at the end of a flowering stalk, and are often surrounded by little bulblets, which gives this plant an unusual and interesting appearance.

Unlike chives, garlic is not typically grown as an indoor plant. Plant garlic cloves in very early spring two inches deep and about six inches apart. Garlic does well in rich, well-cultivated soil in full sun. Cutting back the flowering stalks when they develop in early summer helps bulbs to develop; each clove will multiply during the growing season. In midsummer when the leaves turn yellow and begin to lean toward the ground, lift the entire plant, shake off the soil, and store your bulbs in a dry, dark place.

One way to continue to enjoy garlic through the winter is to dry the flower heads left on some of your plants and use them in dried flower arrangements. Another decorative idea is to make a garlic rope by braiding the dried leaves of a number of bulbs together.

The flavor of garlic is strong, and a single clove enhances stews, soups, sauces, salad dressings, and vinegars. Minced fresh garlic in sweet butter lets you make wonderful garlic bread, and goes well in any dish which garlic bread accompanies. Slivers of garlic in a leg of lamb or steak are a must to garlic lovers.

Twenty-five Useful Herbs

Lemon Balm *Melissa officinalis*

—MINT FAMILY—

The leaves of this herb have a delightful lemony fragrance, and it is perhaps for this reason that an Arab proverb credits lemon balm with making the heart merry and joyful. From the days of the ancient Greeks to Victorian times, it was said to benefit the nervous system, chase away melancholy, and strengthen memory. In fact, an early English herbal recommended balm tea for students to drive away heaviness of mind, sharpen understanding, and increase memory for exams.

Greek physicians used lemon balm to close battle wounds, although Pliny recorded that bleeding was stopped just as well if the herb were applied to the weapon that had caused the wound! Today it is known that oil of lemon balm helps prevent infection, and it is still used in dressing wounds.

According to the ancients, lemon balm could only be picked without mishap if music was played to distract the snakes that always guarded it. Serpents aside, anyone who picks lemon balm usually faces stiff competition from the bees that swarm around its flowers. It has been called the "bee herb," and its name, *Melissa*, is Greek for honeybee. Beekeepers have used it to attract swarms to new hives, and its crushed leaves have been used to soothe bee stings.

Lemon balm is a fairly hardy, strong and bushy perennial that grows to a height of about two feet. Its leaves are thin, heart-shaped, and deeply veined. Like all mints, it has square stems. Its inconspicuous flowers are yellow when budding, but turn white as they open.

Lemon balm is a fine windowsill or container plant. It needs two to three hours of sun a day. Give it moist soil; it is one of the few plants that do well in a pot without drainage holes. As it grows, pinch back the tops to encourage a bushy, compact growth, and enjoy its fragrant scent.

Outdoors, lemon balm does best in moderately rich, moist soil in full sunlight, but it also grows in shade. Like most mints, it spreads like a weed, so wherever you plant it it may grow too well. It is easily started from seed and seedlings grow rapidly. However, it can take more than a month to germinate, so it is often more satisfactory to take stem cuttings or make divisions. Take cuttings in the spring and plant them in full sun about a foot apart; they will root easily. To divide, simply dig up a clump in early spring, cut it apart with a shovel, and replant the pieces you want to keep.

Lemon balm is useful whenever you want the taste of lemon. Use it sparingly in mint sauce, or enjoy it with fish, lamb, beef, salads, and fruit dishes. A crushed leaf immersed for a few minutes in a cold drink gives it a fine lemon flavor.

Lemon Verbena

Lippia citriodora
—VERBENA FAMILY—

Lemon verbena is an herb that can grow more than 20 feet high in its native habitat of the mountains of Chile and Argentina. The entire plant smells of lemon.

It's not surprising that the Spanish conquistadors brought it with them when they returned home, and it became as popular in Europe as in the New World.

It is only hardy outdoors south of Virginia, in localities where temperatures do not drop below 20° F. Elsewhere, it is strictly an indoor plant, and a most satisfactory one. As a container plant it also benefits from occasional applications of a liquid fertilizer. Regular pruning keeps it to a reasonable height and makes it bushier. A weekly wash keeps it free of mites.

If grown in a tub, you can place it outdoors for the summer and bring it indoors before frost. If you live in the South and want to grow it outdoors, choose a warm and sheltered place, water it as you do your other herbs, and fertilize it occasionally.

Young cuttings root well. As lemon verbena sets seed very infrequently, you may want to obtain a summer cutting from a fellow gardener. Alternatively, young plants can be purchased from nurseries.

The long, lemon-scented leaves of lemon verbena can be used wherever a lemon flavor is needed—stuffings, poultry, fish, desserts, fruit drinks, and preserves. It makes a nice tea and can sometimes be used in place of mint.

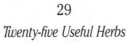

Lovage Levisticum officinale

—CARROT FAMILY—

Like bay and rosemary, lovage is an herb from the Mediterranean region used medicinally by the Greeks and Romans. It became very popular during the Middle Ages as a culinary and medicinal plant. It was cultivated by Charlemagne, and was also commonly grown in medieval monastery gardens. Early herbalists recommended it as a cure for many ailments—red eyes, stomach aches, colic, jaundice, freckles, obesity, flatulence, sore throats and more—a useful plant indeed! Today, people are more interested in the taste of lovage, which resembles celery with a touch of curry.

This herb has smooth, dark green leaves that are deeply cut and almost fernlike, making it an attractive background plant. Stalks shoot up in early summer bearing small yellow blossoms, and, later, aromatic seeds much enjoyed by birds.

Lovage can grow seven or eight feet tall outdoors, so it is not an herb for small gardens. Indoors, it can be grown as a container plant. Give it direct sunlight for several hours each day and cut it back to keep it to a reasonable height of 12 to 15 inches.

Lovage is easy to grow. Because it is a perennial, once started you will have it to enjoy for many years. You can sow the seed in the fall, but since you will probably need only one plant it might be better to start with a few seedlings or a division. In the fall, dig up a plant two or three years old and divide the roots to make more plants.

The seeds, leaves, stems, and roots of lovage are all edible, though the roots are strongly flavored and should be peeled before boiling. Fresh leaves can be used wherever the flavor of celery is desired. Soups, stews, chowders, salads, and meat loaf are all enhanced by fresh lovage. It should be used sparingly, however, because the flavor is stronger than that of celery. For instance, one leaf of lovage flavors enough soup for three or four people. Dried lovage is good in sauces and poultry dressing. The seeds can be used in cakes and breads. Even the hollow stems are useful—they make fine drinking straws!

Marjoram Origanum majorana

—MINT FAMILY—

This herb, also known as sweet marjoram, was a great favorite of the Greeks and Romans, who found it growing freely in the high meadows and hills around the Mediterranean. The Greeks gave it a name that meant "joy of the mountains," and used it in food, perfume, medicine, and as a strewing herb. Through the centuries it has been used and appreciated for its warm and pleasing taste that blends with a variety of foods.

The Greeks and Romans crowned young lovers with garlands of marjoram as a symbol of happiness. It was also believed to ease grief, and was often planted on graves. A good growth of marjoram on a grave indicated that the soul of the deceased was at rest. In later times, herbalists recommended that people sniff sprigs of marjoram to preserve their health. Dairymen laid sprigs of marjoram beside new milk to keep it from curdling during thunderstorms. It was also used to polish furniture.

Marjoram is a compact, bushy plant that grows to about a foot in height. It has gray-green, oval leaves and small, white flowers that grow in knot-like clumps, which suggest another of its common names, knot marjoram.

Marjoram is a fine container plant. From your sunny kitchen windowsill, its aroma will delight you. As you pick leaves for cooking, pinch back growing shoots to keep it to a compact height of about eight inches.

Although perennial, marjoram can only survive the winter in places where there is no frost; farther north it is effectively an annual. Its small seeds are slow to germinate, so you may want to start it indoors in pots and set out clumps of seedlings after any danger of frost. Place the clumps about eight inches apart in a sunny site with well-drained, rich soil. Marjoram is a delicate plant, and benefits from careful weeding while young.

Marjoram has a delicate but surprisingly pervasive flavor that blends especially well with basil, thyme, chives, and parsley. A versatile herb, it is used in meats, fish, poultry, soups, stews, salads, vegetables, egg dishes, macaroni and cheese, sausage, and stuffings—in other words, almost everywhere.

Mints Mentha

—MINT FAMILY—

The fresh, cool taste of mint has made it a favorite through the centuries in many parts of the world. The smell of mint meant strength to the Greeks. They used it extensively in ceremonies and to perfume their baths, and Greek athletes scented their bodies with it. The Athenians went so far as to reserve mint to rub on their weapons to give them extra strength in battle.

In Biblical times, mint was so highly valued that Pharisees could pay their tithes with it. The Romans used mint as a strewing herb, rubbed it on tables as a sign of hospitality, put it in their baths, ate it to comfort and strengthen their nerves, and invented mint sauce. It seems to have fallen out of use with the decay of the Empire, however, for the crusaders discovered mint all over again and brought it back to Europe. There was a place for mint in the herb gardens of the medieval monasteries; it was used to clear the head, quicken the senses, and as a hair wash and tooth whitener. When the colonists came to the New World, mints were among their herbal supplies.

Mints belong to a large family that encompasses many other herbs. Part of their great attraction is their range of fragrances—mint, but also apple, pineapple, and lemon.

All mints do well in sunny or shaded spots with rich, moist soil. Mints are fine container plants, and do very well indoors with only two to three hours of sun. They are notorious for their creeping roots, which can spread in every direction and crowd out everything else in a bed. For this reason, you should grow your mints in separate containers. Unlike other herbs, which require good drainage, mints seem to like having their feet wet and can be grown in containers without drainage holes. Water them often, but don't overdo it. Trim your plants back frequently to keep them at a height of eight or 10 inches.

If planting mint in your yard, surround it with a metal strip to a depth of at least 10 inches to keep its roots from spreading out of control. Mints are strong growers and should be kept well fertilized. Because they are such strong growers, they must be divided and repotted every couple of years.

The different varieties of mints hybridize readily with each other, so it is best to use root divisions to ensure you get the plant you want, since seeds do not necessarily produce offspring which resemble the parent plant. Mint is much easier to start from root divisions than from seed, but if you want to try growing mint from seed, the germination time is about two weeks. Young plants should be thinned to about eight inches apart. Luckily, anyone with a bed of mint is almost sure to have plenty and is happy to give clumps of it away to friends, neighbors, or perfect strangers.

There are many kinds of mint. Some of the most popular are:

Mentha spicata—This species, spearmint, is one of the most common and has the longest history of use. Its smooth, bright green leaves are narrow, pointed, and have sharp teeth along their edges. It can grow to two or three feet, but tends to be rather sprawling.

Mentha aquatica var. *crispa*—This is another spearmint-flavored variety. Its heart-shaped, crinkled leaves make it an attractive garnish.

Mentha piperita—This species has the strongest peppermint taste, and is probably a natural cross between water mint and spearmint. A tea made from this mint is a traditional remedy for upset stomachs.

Mentha suaveolens—This species is known as apple mint because of its fragrance. The leaves are soft and round, with a down that has given it the name of "woolly mint."

Mentha suaveolens 'Variegata'—A distinct pineapple fragrance distinguishes this mint. It has a striking appearance, its green leaves dappled with creamy white.

Mentha piperita X *citrata*—This mint is characterized by a citrus fragrance that seems to intensify the scents of other nearby herbs. Its young leaves are heart-shaped and edged with purple.

Fresh mint leaves are used in salads, desserts, and garnishes. Mint sauce is a must with roast lamb, and goes well with fish. Mint makes good jelly. Experimenting with all the varieties provides an interesting assortment of vinegars. Mint adds a refreshing taste to cold drinks and new zest to pea soup. And, of course, there's always the famous mint julep.

Oregano   *Origanum vulgare*

—MINT FAMILY—

Oregano, also known as wild marjoram, is related to marjoram, but it has a more pungent flavor. Like marjoram, it is native to the mountains and hills that border the Mediterranean. The Greeks and Romans often used it as a tasty addition to many foods. It is said that the meat of goats which feed on it becomes delicately flavored.

Oregano can be grown from cuttings, root divisions, or seed. The advantage of the first two methods is that you can select material from a plant already known to be flavorful. Some varieties of this herb are definitely superior to the wild species. *Origanum vulgare* 'Viride' is a particularly good variety which may be available at local nurseries.

Oregano is an excellent indoor plant. If kept under lights and at about 70° F, it germinates in about four days. Pinch off growing shoots as you gather leaves for cooking to keep it to a reasonable height.

Outdoors, sow the seed in early spring in a sunny spot. Press it very lightly into the soil, so that it isn't covered by the soil. Seed will germinate in about three weeks. This perennial can grow up to three feet in height, so thin young plants to about a foot apart.

Although long a staple herb in Greece and Italy, oregano was not well known here until after World War II. Now it is famous as an essential ingredient of pizza and many other dishes. Its flavor resembles that of marjoram, but is stronger with minty overtones.

Parsley *Petroselinum crispum*

—CARROT FAMILY—

Parsley is a well-known culinary herb too often over-looked. The Greeks valued parsley for its symbolic significance, but never used it in cooking. In-stead, Greek charioteers fed it to their horses to give them stam-ina, believing that the horses of the gods fed on parsley. It was used in wreaths to crown victorious athletes be-cause Hercules was said to have used it in his garlands. Parsley was also placed on banquet tables and worn as wreaths around the necks of diners, but its function was to prevent drunkenness; it was thought that intoxicating fumes were absorbed by the herb's fragrance. Interestingly, it was also served between courses and chewed to cleanse the breath of garlic and onion odors. From this early practice comes our traditional use of parsley as a garnish. It is a well-recognized breath freshener to this day.

By medieval times, parsley was used in cooking and commonly grown in monastery gardens. Because it is unusually slow to germinate, the belief arose that it had to go to the Devil and back seven times before it could sprout. Perhaps because of this it was traditionally planted on Good Friday to ensure a good harvest.

Parsley is a biennial, taking two seasons to reach full growth and produce seeds. Since only the leaves are used, most growers consider it an annual. It is not difficult to grow, and does well in rich, moist soil and in sun or partial shade. It does need plenty of water, especially when young.

Parsley is a wonderful indoor plant. It thrives in a sunny kitchen windowsill box, or deep pot that leaves room for its long taproot. Cut and use outside leaves, and keep the plant about eight inches tall.

Outdoors, seed should be sown early in spring to give it plenty of time to germinate. A preliminary overnight soaking helps. Thin young plants to about eight inches apart. Parsley grows about a foot by the end of its first season, and produces a full crop of dark green, finely-divided leaves. Although the curly-leaved *Petroselinum crispum* is most commonly grown, the flatter-leaved Italian parsley, *P. hortense*, is becoming increasingly popular.

An interesting way to make sure you have fresh parsley

all winter long is to dig up the roots of some parsley plants in the fall and replant the largest ones indoors in pots of sand. Water them occasionally. The roots, using the reserves of food stored during the summer, will continue to send up new green shoots for the rest of the winter. In spring, discard them and start new plants from seed.

Parsley is one of the few herbs that keeps its flavor and food value when oven-dried. To do this, spread the leaves on a pan in a thin layer and dry them in a 400° F oven for five minutes, turning them over halfway through. The crisp leaves can be crumbled through a coarse screen and stored in a tightly closed jar. Both fresh and dried leaves can be used with meats, fish, poultry, soups, salads, casseroles, omelets, sauces, creamed vegetables, stews, and eggs. The fresh leaves are always useful as a garnish.

Rosemary *Rosmarinus officinalis*
—MINT FAMILY—

This is perhaps the most satisfactory of all herbs for a sunny kitchen windowsill—in the sun's warmth, its fragrance pervades the entire room.

Rosemary grows wild as a small shrub on the shores of the Mediterranean. Often, when the wind is right, its spicy pine scent carries far out to sea. Its name, *Rosmarinus*, means "dew of the sea," perhaps because its pale blue blossoms resemble dewdrops on their branches. There is a legend that the flowers became blue after the Virgin Mary put her blue cloak over a rosemary shrub while fleeing to Egypt.

In ancient Greece, this plant was believed to strengthen memory. Students would twine rosemary in their hair when studying for exams. Rosemary was also a symbol of remembrance of the dead, and a reminder of friendship and faithfulness to the living. It often formed part of the bridal wreath and was given to

The Windowsill Herb Garden

wedding guests—and also to the bridegroom, to remind him to be faithful.

Greek and Roman physicians used rosemary for many ailments. For example, it was believed that a bag of rosemary leaves in bath water strengthened the sinews of the bather. Its legendary association with Mary also gave this herb a role as a protector against evil. In medieval times, it was used as a charm against the evil eye and was placed in cradles to protect children from nightmares. Burned in churches as incense, it was also considered a defense against witchcraft. It was even said that rosemary would refuse to grow in the gardens of the wicked, which may have caused some gardeners anxious moments! In a more worldly vein, the Elizabethans used rosemary to beautify hair and prevent baldness. To this day it is an ingredient of some hair oils.

Rosemary is a shrubby perennial that, in its native habitat, can grow to five feet in height. With its smooth, dark green, needlelike leaves it looks rather like a miniature fir tree. Dwarf and creeping varieties can grace even the smallest of gardens.

Rosemary can be grown indoors with less light than many herbs. Give it a little lime in its soil, and regular feedings with light fertilizer. It should be kept moist and misted often; if allowed to dry out, it will die.

Outdoors, grow rosemary in a sunny spot with well-drained soil and keep it well watered. If the soil is acid, sweeten it with a little lime. The seeds of rosemary are hard to germinate, and the plants grow very slowly. Cuttings or young plants from your local nursery are usually more satisfactory. If your area has cold winters, be prepared to take your plants inside, since this herb is not hardy below 15° F.

Most meats and poultry taste better with rosemary. It is also good in soups, stuffings, sauces, salad dressings, and vegetables. It is especially recommended as an addition to baking-powder biscuits.

Twenty-five Useful Herbs

Sage *Salvia officinalis*
—MINT FAMILY—

Sage is an essential ingredient of stuffing, without which no holiday turkey would be complete. Its importance to the ancients, however, was medicinal and almost miraculous. It was believed to prevent the decay of aging and preserve the vigor of youth. By the tenth century there was a saying, "Why should a man die who grows sage in his garden?"

The name *Salvia* comes from the Latin for healthy or well, and during the Middle Ages this herb had a multitude of health-related uses. For example, it was believed to quicken the senses, clear the mind, improve memory and vision, and prevent colds. It was also used to ease rheumatism, ulcers, sore throats, and tuberculosis.

Sage makes a very acceptable tea that was so preferred in seventeenth-century China that some Dutch traders made fortunes by trading sage for Chinese tea—at the rate of four bales of Chinese tea for one of sage! During the Revolutionary War, Americans drank sage tea during the embargo on British tea. Sage was also said to aid the digestion of fats, so it became customary to garnish roast duck or goose with a sprig of sage for diners to nibble on, a precursor to its current enormous popularity as a stuffing for all kinds of poultry.

Sage is a neat, shrubby perennial that can grow up to two and a half feet tall. Some of the many interesting varieties available are shorter and make excellent border plants. The broad, deeply veined leaves have a pebbly surface and are a distinctive shade of gray-green—sage green, in fact. The attractive spikes of bluish-lavender flowers are loved by bees.

Sage is a hardy plant. It thrives in sun and well-drained, rather limy soil. It is easily grown from seed or cuttings. Its germination rate is low, so plant sage seed densely.

Indoors, give sage three to four hours of sun daily, and add a little lime to its soil. Water it thoroughly, but allow the soil to dry before watering again. Wash your plants once a month, and pinch them back to keep them bushy and compact.

To grow sage outdoors, sow the seed once the soil has warmed in the spring, or start your plants indoors in early spring and then transplant them. Thin young plants to about a foot apart. Sage should be divided and replanted every three to four years. It can withstand temperatures as low as −20° F, so it is a hardy perennial over much of North America.

An interesting way to grow sage is to bury the end of a branch. It will root and form a small plant that can eventually be cut away from the parent.

A strong herb, sage has a pungent, somewhat lemony taste and can be used sparingly. Combine it with marjoram and thyme to add the ideal flavor to stuffings. It is also good for sausage, soups, sauces, dressings, and cheese dishes, as well as tea.

Salad Burnet Sanguisorba minor
—ROSE FAMILY—

Salad burnet resembles borage in flavor and usage. Its Greek name, *poterium*, came from its use in wine cups. Like borage, burnet was recommended for a merry heart for many centuries. During the Middle Ages it was an ingredient of an herb mixture used against the plague. Its chief medicinal use, however, has been as an astringent to encourage the closing of wounds; it is still used as an astringent.

The toothed, fernlike leaves of this perennial herb form a flat rosette close to the ground, but its flowering stems can grow up to three feet tall. Reddish flowers appear in thimble-shaped heads during a plant's second year.

Burnet grows well indoors or out as a container plant and needs very little care. Indoors, give it at least four hours of sun daily and a deep pot to accommodate its long taproot. Water it when it feels dry. It thrives in full sun and ordinary to poor soil. It is easily grown from seed.

Outdoors, sow burnet in its permanent location, since its long taproot does not transplant well. Plants started outdoors in late summer can be moved indoors for the winter. Although salad burnet is a hardy perennial, its young leaves are the most tender, so you may want to resow this easily grown plant each year.

Burnet tastes like cucumber. Just like borage, its fresh leaves can be used in salads and cold drinks. Dried leaves are a good addition to salad dressings and soups.

Savory   Satureja hortensis and S. montana

—MINT FAMILY—

Satureja hortensis (summer savory) is an annual, but *S. montana* (winter savory) is a perennial. Their flavors are similar, but winter savory's is stronger.

Both savories are native to the Mediterranean region, and were known to the Greeks and Romans. The Latin name, *Satureja*, is derived from the word for satyr. These mythical creatures, half man and half goat, were believed to hold savory in high regard. Perhaps this is why summer savory long enjoyed a reputation as an aphrodisiac.

The savories have a long culinary history. The Greeks and Romans blended them with thyme for soups and stuffings, and used them in sauces for meat and fish. They were brought to Britain by the Romans, and were grown in Charlemagne's herb gardens.

Savories have uses other than culinary. Crushed leaves of summer savory have been used since ancient times to soothe the pain of bee and wasp stings. Savories have been recommended to cure deafness and indigestion. Savories were once eaten by fat people in the belief that this would help them grow thin.

Summer and winter savory are easily grown from cuttings or seed. Summer savory germinates more quickly than winter. Plant savory shallowly, and press the soil gently over the seeds. Savory does best in full sun and average soil.

Both savories do well indoors as container plants. Give them several hours of sun a day and a bit of lime in the soil. Water whenever the soil feels dry. Trim them back to control their tendency to sprawl.

Summer savory needs more moisture than winter savory, and grows taller and more spindly. Trim back its tips to encourage branching. Winter savory can be trimmed into a low hedge to edge a border most attractively.

Summer savory goes especially well with beans, and is known in many countries as the "bean herb." It is also one of the great blending herbs and goes well with almost everything. Use it with meats, fish, poultry, salads, stuffings, sauces, soups, gravies, meat loaf, and egg dishes. Winter savory can be used whenever summer savory is called for, but keep in mind its strength and use it sparingly.

Sorrel Rumex scutatus
—BUCKWHEAT FAMILY—

Sorrel was used by the Egyptians and Romans to counteract the richness of other foods; the Romans often ate it as a precursor to their heavy main meals. It was commonly grown in European vegetable gardens from the Middle Ages to the eighteenth century, but it escaped because it sets seed easily, and became very widely naturalized. A rather lovely belief was that the cuckoo ate this plant to clear its voice for singing.

Commonly known as French sorrel, this species is the one most used in cooking. Its close relative, garden sorrel (*Rumex acetosa*), is also used in cooking.

Sorrel is a hardy perennial. Its arrow-shaped leaves have an intriguing, rather lemony taste. Garden sorrel's leaves are best when full grown. They can be bitter in the heat of midsummer, but are milder and delicious in spring and fall. French sorrel is an especially good spring green.

Sorrel is an excellent indoor plant that needs as much sun as possible. Grow it in a south-facing window to give it at least four to five hours of sunlight daily. Give it plenty of water, a deep pot for its long taproot, and fertilize it every couple of weeks. It grows about eight inches tall.

Outdoors, plant French sorrel in well-drained soil in full sun. Garden sorrel can grow in partial shade. Thin seedlings to about six inches apart.

Sorrel is traditionally used in soups and in sauces for fish.

Tarragon *Artemisia dracunculus*

—DAISY FAMILY—

Unlike many herbs, tarragon seems to have been virtually unknown to the Greeks, although Pliny recorded that it prevented fatigue. This belief persisted through the Middle Ages, when pilgrims traveling to the Holy Land tucked leaves of tarragon into their sandals to sustain them on the long journey.

Tarragon was also valued as an antidote to the bites of small dragons. Tarragon's roots are dense and tangled, and must have resembled coiling serpents or dragons to medieval imaginations. Any plant so resembling a dragon was certainly expected to supply a remedy for its bite! The name *dracunculus* means "little dragon," and the common name tarragon is derived from the French word for this mythical creature. By extension, tarragon was also held to be good for the bites of serpents and venomous insects.

By Charlemagne's time, tarragon was appreciated as a culinary herb. It did not reach England until several

The Windowsill Herb Garden

centuries later, during the Tudor era. At first it was grown only in royal gardens, but today it is indispensable to French cookery.

Tarragon is a bushy perennial that grows two or three feet tall. Its leaves are smooth, dark green, and narrow, and release an odor of anise when crushed. The tiny, loosely clustered, greenish-white flowers do not usually set seed.

Tarragon cannot be grown from seed. Since cuttings root very slowly, root division is the easiest way to get new plants. In the spring, lift a clump of a tarragon with a spading fork, carefully pull apart the tangle of roots, and replant. Discard dead or woody pieces. Do this every three or four years to give the crowded roots more room to grow.

This fine indoor plant thrives in your sunniest location. Be sure to provide good drainage. Water when the surface of the soil feels dry, but do not overwater. Feed about twice a month. Its famous tangled roots grow very rapidly in good conditions, so you may have to transplant to a larger pot two or three times a year. An indoor pot of tarragon grows about a foot tall.

Chew a pinch of tarragon leaves. After a moment, the anise taste disappears and is followed by a warm, numbing sensation. Arab physicians once took advantage of this by giving their patients a leaf of tarragon to chew so that their tongues would be too numb to taste a dose of bitter medicine.

Outdoors, place your plants about two feet apart in a sunny location with well-drained, loamy soil. Good drainage is more essential to tarragon than to most other herbs. Tarragon is hardy in temperatures down to about 10° F, but should be mulched with leaves or straw during the winter in colder climates.

The taste of tarragon is distinctive and individual. Although it is an ingredient of French *fines herbes*, it is usually used alone. It is used to flavor fish sauces, tartar sauce, mayonnaise, vinegar, and pickles. It is also good with steaks, chops, poultry, salads, soups, vegetables, and egg dishes.

An interesting way to use tarragon is to place some fresh leaves in a wide-mouthed jar. Pour red vinegar heated almost to the boiling point over the leaves. The vinegar becomes tarragon vinegar. The leaves can be removed, rinsed, and used as fresh.

Thyme *Thymus vulgaris*

—MINT FAMILY—

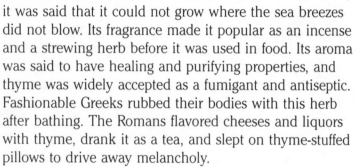

Thyme is one of the many members of the mint family. It comes from around the edges of the Mediterranean, and it was said that it could not grow where the sea breezes did not blow. Its fragrance made it popular as an incense and a strewing herb before it was used in food. Its aroma was said to have healing and purifying properties, and thyme was widely accepted as a fumigant and antiseptic. Fashionable Greeks rubbed their bodies with this herb after bathing. The Romans flavored cheeses and liquors with thyme, drank it as a tea, and slept on thyme-stuffed pillows to drive away melancholy.

During the Middle Ages, as in the days of the Greeks, thyme was the symbol of courage. Knights riding off to the Crusades often carried embroidered scarves depicting a bee hovering over a sprig of thyme. Thyme was worn by young girls to encourage their suitors, and a soup made with thyme and beer was said to overcome shyness.

Herbalists wrote that thyme strengthened the lungs, cured gout, banished dullness of sight, kept away nightmares, warded off colds, and healed coughs. The usefulness of thyme for coughs and colds continues to this day. Its essential oil, thymol, has antibacterial properties and is used in many cough medicines.

Thyme is a sturdy, low-growing perennial with spreading, woody stems which bear small gray-green leaves shaped like arrowheads. It seldom grows taller than eight to 10 inches, but its many branches thickly covered with leaves give it a pleasant, bushy appearance. It flowers in summer, and its light pink or lavender blossoms are extremely attractive to bees. It is said that you can hear a field where wild thyme grows long before you can see it from the humming of bees. The famous honey of Mt. Hymettus owes its flavor to wild thyme.

A closely related variety known as lemon thyme (*Thymus citriodorus*) has a strong lemon scent, and is becoming increasingly popular as a culinary herb.

Thyme is a very satisfactory container or windowbox plant. Give it a lot of sun and occasional feedings. It does not do well in low humidity, so if the air in your house is dry, your plants will benefit from a nearby pan of water. Water your plants when the soil surface feels dry, and wash the leaves from time to time. Drooping branches should be trimmed for a neat appearance.

Outdoors, thyme does well in average to poor soil, but it must have good drainage or it will succumb to fungal diseases. It also needs at least half a day of sun. It can be grown from seed, but must be started indoors at a temperature of about 70° F. Cuttings or root divisions may be more satisfactory. Thin young plants to about eight inches apart, and weed them carefully. You can also let a naturally drooping branch of a mature plant take root to form a new plant that can eventually be cut away from the parent.

Thyme is a useful herb with the happy ability to get along well with almost anything. Its flavor is strong, however, so use it sparingly. Fresh leaves are good for salads and vinegars. Dried thyme seasons meats, poultry, fish, chowders, soups, sauces, gravies, cheese dishes, and stuffing.

46

The Windowsill Herb Garden

Cooking with Herbs

*H*erbs are nature's gift to any cook. When used with a discriminating hand, they enhance foods with their flavors and fragrances, rather than overwhelm. The trick is knowing when to use them and how much to use.

The best way to become acquainted with an herb is to start with a leaf or a small piece. Press and rub the leaf between two fingers to release the oil. Then take a sniff and try a nibble. Add a few leaves to a cup of broth and sniff. You'll soon learn that some herbs, such as chives, parsley, chervil, and summer savory, can be used almost anywhere. Others, such as basil, dill, mint, tarragon, and thyme, tend to stand out and should be mixed with less assertive herbs. Still others, such as rosemary, sage, oregano, and winter savory, are strongly pungent and should be used sparingly.

Cooking with herbs is not difficult. Keep in mind that herbs are meant to enhance flavors, not overpower them, so use a light touch.

Gathering and Storing Fresh Herbs

One of the nice things about growing your own herbs is that you can pick a few leaves from your plants any time you need them. You also can harvest and store them for year-round enjoyment.

Herbs are at their peak when just beginning to bloom. The best time to gather herbs is early in the morning. The oil content of the leaves is the highest at this time, and the more oil, the more flavor. If you are harvesting entire plants, pull up or cut down the annuals, leaving a few for seed. Take only the top half of perennials so that they can continue to build strength to survive the winter.

It's important to process your herbs quickly; they begin to lose their volatile oils and diminish in flavor as soon as they are cut. Rinse them in cool water and gently pat dry with paper towels. Be sure to discard any damaged leaves.

You can store fresh herbs in your refrigerator for about a week by putting their stems in a jar containing at least an inch of water and covering it loosely with a plastic bag. Smaller herb sprigs can be wrapped in a paper towel, sealed in a plastic bag, and refrigerated for about a week. To store fresh herbs for longer periods, you should dry or freeze them.

Drying Herbs

To dry herbs, first remove any dead or wilted leaves. Wash the plants gently but thoroughly in cool water, and gently blot them as dry as possible between paper towels. Separate them into bunches and tie the stems of each bunch together. Place each bunch in a paper (not plastic) bag, and secure the mouth as loosely as possible around the stem end. This will protect the herbs from dust and light while they dry. Hang your herbs in a dry, well-ventilated place (an attic is ideal) with a temperature range of 70° to 90° F.

After a week or two, shake your bags and listen for a dry rustle. The leaves should be dry enough to crumble at a touch when you take them out of the bags. If they are not absolutely dry they can become moldy later, and if they are left too long they may start to reabsorb water. If you have any doubts, dry the leaves for a few minutes in a warm oven (less than 100° F).

When you are satisfied that the leaves are dry, strip

them from their stalks, put them in clean, dry containers, and store them in a cool, dry place. They will keep their flavor for a year or more.

Drying herbs in your microwave oven is not recommended. The leaves dry in just a few seconds and may flame, causing a fire in your oven.

While the shelf over the stove may be very convenient, it's about the worst possible place to keep herbs! Preserve the strength of dried herbs by storing them away from the heat of the range, refrigerator exhaust vents, or under-cabinet lighting.

It's a good idea to check the potency of your dried herbs from time to time. Do this by giving them the "sniff test." Quickly pass open containers by your nose; if you can't identify the aroma, it's best to discard that herb.

The flavor of dried herbs is more concentrated than that of fresh. You'll need about three times as much of a fresh herb to give you the same flavor intensity as its dried counterpart. If you substitute dried herbs for fresh, start with one-third the amount of fresh herbs suggested in the recipe. Taste—if the flavor is not strong enough, just add a little more.

Freezing Herbs

Although textures will be slightly softer and colors may fade, flavors remain wonderfully fresh when herbs are frozen. First, rinse herbs in cool water. Shake off excess water and carefully pat dry with paper towels. Prior to freezing, remove stems from stemmed herbs such as basil, mint, oregano, tarragon, and sage.

Lay the leaves in a single layer on a baking sheet and freeze for several hours. When the herbs are frozen, place them in freezer containers or heavy plastic bags. Label all packages with the herb name and date. To keep them from getting crushed, be sure not to place heavy containers on top of your bags of herbs, or keep them all in one large plastic container. Herbs will keep in your freezer for a year or more.

Basil is an exception. It must be blanched before freezing because it turns black when frozen. To blanch, place leaves in boiling water for just one second. Remove immediately and drain on paper towels until cool.

Cooking with Herbs

Using Herbs

To cut up small amounts of fresh herbs quickly, place the leaves in a deep, glass measuring cup and snip with kitchen shears.

Use a food processor to chop more than three tablespoons of herbs.

To easily remove herbs from stews or soups, wrap them in cheesecloth to make a spice bag, or use a tea ball to encase them. Before serving, remove the spice bag with a slotted spoon and discard.

When chopping fresh herbs, use a very sharp knife to release their flavors.

Fresh or dried herbs have a stronger flavor if crushed before being added to food. Use a mortar and pestle or a wooden spoon and the side of a bowl, or crush the herbs between your fingers.

For the best flavor in long-cooking pot roasts, soups, and stews, add fresh herbs during the last 20 minutes of cooking.

Fresh herbs sometimes do not have a chance to release their flavors in salad dressings, cold sauces, marinades, and some microwave recipes. Be sure to taste these dishes and add more herbs if necessary.

To store basil or sage for longer periods in your refrigerator, layer the leaves in a jar and cover with a light olive or vegetable oil. These delicate herbs may discolor slightly, but you'll be able to keep them for a couple of months. The oil picks up their flavor, so save it to use in cooking or salad dressings.

You can avoid crunchy dried flecks in your sauces by rehydrating dried herbs in boiling water, then draining them.

To give a dried herb fresh color, add an equal amount of minced fresh parsley.

Seasoning and flavoring food is mostly a matter of personal preference. The following chart is a guide to using fresh herbs. After the chart, you'll find a collection of recipes using both fresh and dried herbs.

Herbs to Enhance Every Dish

You should generally use about 2 to 3 tablespoons minced fresh herbs or ½ to 1 teaspoon dried herbs in recipes that serve four people. Use herbs sparingly at first; you can always add more. Sometimes a single herb will accomplish your desired flavor, and other times you may wish to use a combination of herbs.

Herb	*Choices*
Basil—A green, leafy herb with strong flavor and aroma. The leaves are delicate, so handle with care.	Use in vinegars, pesto, and tomato sauces, and with vegetables, fish, sauces, poultry, eggs, and salads.
Bay—Has a strong but warm, pungent flavor. Leaf must be removed before serving. The fresher the leaf, the stronger the flavor.	Use for soups, stews, fish, vegetables, and milk pudding. Bay leaf is the essential ingredient of *Bouquet Garni.*
Borage—Young leaves taste like cucumber, and blue flowers add startling color to recipes.	Use in salads, dressings, sauces, and beverages.
Burnet—Has a cucumber flavor when fresh, and nutty when dried.	Use in green salads, butters, vinegars, dips, and as a garnish.
Catnip—Feathery, heart-shaped leaves have a distinctive flavor and aroma.	Use in teas. Said to aid digestion.
Chervil—Feathery leaves have a delicate anise or tarragon aroma and a peppery, parsley-like flavor.	Use for soups, vegetables, chicken, fish, stuffings, and sauces. Makes an excellent herb vinegar.
Cilantro—Distinctive pungent flavor. Use sparingly. Similar in appearance to parsley.	Widely used in Mexican, Chinese, and South American cuisines. Chop and sprinkle in sauces, soups, and salads.

Herb	Choices	Herb	Choices
Cress—Strong peppery, crisp flavor. Only use fresh. Can be chopped and frozen with a little water in ice cube trays.	Use in soups, salad dressings, sandwiches, and with cheese, fish, and poultry. Try cress in a quiche in place of spinach.	**Lemon Balm**—Heart-shaped leaves have a citrus flavor.	Use with fish, pork, chicken, beverages, herb butters, salads, and fruit.
Dill—Considered indispensable by Scandinavian cooks. Enhances flavors without overpowering them.	Use for biscuits, vegetables, fish, soup, salads, vinegars, and pickles. Seeds are used in pickles and breads.	**Lemon Verbena**—Fragrant, with subtle lemon flavor. Dries well; flavor intensifies when dried.	Use in jellies, salad dressings, desserts, salads, and beverages.
Fennel—Versatile herb with a distinctive licorice flavor.	Use chopped leaves in dips, salads, and soups, and with fish and chicken.	**Lovage**—Flavor similar to celery. Use leaves and stalks.	Use in soups, stuffing, gravy, and stews.
Garlic—Unique flavor and aroma. Said to aid digestion. Break into cloves, peel, and discard transparent skin. Chop, mince, or crush cloves. Do not overcook (brown); flavor becomes bitter.	Use in Mediterranean dishes and soups, stews, sauces, dips, and just about anywhere except sweet bakery treats.	**Marjoram**—Small, grayish leaves have an exceptionally spicy-sweet flavor. Use in place of sage in many recipes.	Use with fish, chicken, vegetables, eggs, and in soups, stews, and sauces.
		Mint—Cooling and sweet flavors: spearmint and peppermint, as well as apple, orange, and lemon mint.	Use in jellies, salads, beverages, and sauces, and with tomatoes, lamb, and veal.

The Windowsill Herb Garden

Herb	Choices	Herb	Choices
Oregano—Strong, aromatic flavor. Widely used in Italian cuisines.	Use for tomato-based sauces, vegetables, beef, stews, and fish.	**Savory (summer and winter)**—Slight peppery flavor with a subtle sweet spiciness. Sometimes called the "bean herb." Use sparingly.	Use in soups, bean or grain dishes, vegetables, rice, and with poultry.
Parsley—Fresh flavor and clean taste. Flat-leaf parsley has more flavor.	Most widely used herb in every dish except desserts.		
Rosemary—has pine needle-shaped leaves and is one of the most potent herbs. Requires at least 10 minutes of cooking time to release flavor. Flavor is best when cooked.	Use with lamb and potatoes, and in stews, poultry, and vinegars.	**Sorrel**—Spinach-like greens have a sour, tangy flavor. Use fresh only.	Use in soups, salads, sauces, and as a garnish.
		Tarragon—Slender, dark leaves have a spicy, mixed flavor of mint and anise.	Use in sauces and salad dressings. Enhances poultry and shellfish.
Sage—Silvery oval leaves have a warm, slightly bitter taste. Use sparingly.	Use in dressings, sausage, cheese spreads, and with pork, veal, chicken, lamb, and tomatoes.	**Thyme**—Mild but pungent flavor similar to cloves. Can be used liberally. Blends well with other herbs.	Use in soups, chowders, dips, vinegars, fish, vegetables, and jellies. Lemon thyme gives two flavors at once.

Naturally Good Recipes

Whenfresh basil, oregano, or another herb is flourishing in a windowsill, how can any cook resist plucking a few leaves for favorite dishes?

The aroma of herbs invites you to taste them, and their flavors will suggest to you many ways to use them. Whether you're tossing a salad or roasting a leg of lamb, adding herbs can give any recipe flair.

Here are 67 ideas for using herbs with appetizers, soups, salads, vegetables, main dishes, sauces, and desserts.

Appetizers and Soups

Herbs can take center stage as the main ingredients when it comes to flavoring appetizers. For a quick dip, just chop a few tablespoons of your favorite herb and add it to a cup of sour cream or yogurt. To make a simple spread for crackers, add chopped herbs to softened cream cheese. To decorate a wedge of cheese, spread the top and sides with a thin layer of mayonnaise, then press herb leaves into the mayonnaise.

For soups, choose herbs which blend well with all of the other ingredients. Remember to add dried herbs to soups before simmering, and fresh herbs during the last 20 minutes.

Eggplant Caviar

1 large eggplant, about
    1½ pounds
Lemon juice
¼ cup olive oil
2 cloves garlic, chopped
½ cup walnuts
½ cup pecans
1 cup dairy sour cream

5 tablespoons fresh
    chervil, minced
2 dashes cayenne pepper
Salt
2 tablespoons poppy seed
Crusty French bread,
    thinly sliced

Cut a lengthwise slice, about 1 inch thick, from one side of eggplant. Scoop out pulp, leaving ¼-inch shell. Rub shell with lemon juice. Cover and set aside.

Heat olive oil in large skillet over medium-high heat. Cook eggplant pulp and garlic 15 minutes, or until eggplant is tender and lightly browned. Remove from heat.

Place walnuts and pecans in food processor bowl with metal blade. Cover and process until nuts are chopped. Add cooked eggplant; process until smooth.

Add sour cream, chervil, pepper, and 1 tablespoon lemon juice; process until smooth. Taste and season with salt. Stir in poppy seed.

Spoon poppy seed mixture into reserved shell. Cover and refrigerate at least 3 hours to blend flavors.

Keeps up to 4 days in refrigerator. Let stand 1 hour at room temperature before serving. Serve with bread. Makes 2½ cups.

Goat Cheese Marinated with Fresh Sage and Garlic

10 ounces Montrachet goat cheese or other fresh, mild goat cheese

16 to 20 large fresh sage leaves

2 cloves garlic, slivered

12 to 15 black peppercorns, cracked

¾ cup virgin olive oil

Crisp French bread, thinly sliced

Cut cheese into ⅜-inch slices. Arrange half of sage leaves, garlic, and peppercorns on serving dish just large enough to hold the cheese. Arrange sliced cheese on top of sage mixture. Top with remaining sage leaves, garlic, and peppercorns. Drizzle olive oil over cheese.

Cover and refrigerate at least 24 hours.

Let stand at room temperature about 1 hour before serving. Serve with bread. Makes 6 to 8 appetizer servings.

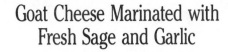

Green Bean Paté with Basil

1 tablespoon vegetable
  oil
1 medium onion,
  chopped
½ pound green beans,
  cooked
3 tablespoons fresh basil,
  chopped
3 hard-cooked eggs

1 teaspoon lemon rind,
  grated
Mayonnaise
Salt
Pepper
Melba toast or crackers
Nasturtium flowers or
  basil sprigs

Heat oil in medium skillet over medium heat. Cook onion until tender. Cool.

Place cooked onion, beans, basil, eggs, and lemon rind in food processor bowl with metal blade. Cover and process until just puréed.

Spoon into bowl. Add enough mayonnaise to hold mixture together. Season with salt and pepper to taste.

Cover and refrigerate until well chilled.

Arrange crackers or Melba toast around paté. Garnish with nasturtium flowers or basil sprigs. Makes 2 cups.

Garlic-Herb Cheese Spread

1 cup ricotta or farmer
  cheese
8 ounces cream cheese,
  softened and cut up
2 cloves garlic, minced
3 tablespoons chopped
  fresh herbs (mar-
  joram, oregano,
  rosemary, sage,
  savory, or thyme)
2 tablespoons fresh basil,
  chopped

1 tablespoon fresh
  chervil or chives,
  chopped
¼ teaspoon pepper
1 teaspoon Worcester-
  shire sauce
¼ teaspoon hot pepper
  sauce
Fresh herb sprigs
Assorted crackers

Place first 9 ingredients in blender container or food processor with metal blade. Cover and process until smooth.

Cover and refrigerate at least one hour. Garnish with fresh herb sprigs and serve with crackers. Makes 2 cups.

Tomato-Dill Bisque

3 tablespoons butter or margarine
1 medium onion, chopped
1 clove garlic, minced
5 medium tomatoes (2 pounds), peeled, seeded, and chopped
1 cup chicken broth

2 teaspoons chopped fresh dill weed or ¾ teaspoon dried dill weed
½ teaspoon sugar
¼ teaspoon celery salt
⅛ teaspoon pepper
½ cup milk
Fresh dill sprigs

Melt butter in 3-quart saucepan over medium-high heat. Add onion and garlic; cook until onion is tender.

Stir in tomatoes and remaining ingredients except milk and dill sprigs. Bring to a boil, then reduce heat to low. Cover and simmer 10 minutes. Cool slightly.

Cover and refrigerate at least 12 hours, or until well chilled.

Place half of the tomato mixture in blender container. Cover and blend at high speed until smooth.

Pour into bowl. Repeat with remaining tomato mixture. Stir in milk.

To serve, ladle soup into bowls. Garnish with dill sprigs. Makes 4 (1-cup) servings.

Black and White Bean Soup with Savory

1 pound dried black beans, rinsed
1 pound dried white beans, rinsed
12 medium cloves garlic
10 to 12 summer savory sprigs, minced, or 1½ to 2 teaspoons crumbled dried savory

½ cup virgin olive oil
6 tablespoons red wine vinegar
4 large jalapeño peppers, seeded and minced
Salt
Nasturtium flowers

Place black beans in bowl and cover with water. Repeat with white beans. Let beans stand overnight to soak.

continued on next page

59

Naturally Good Recipes

Rinse and drain beans separately. Place black and white beans in separate pots and cover with 3 inches of water. Bring both pots of beans to a boil over high heat.

Reduce heat to low. Cover and simmer 1½ hours, or until beans are tender.

Add half of the garlic, savory, and oil to each pot of beans. Add vinegar and peppers to black beans. Let cool a few minutes until easy to handle.

Purée each pot of beans in food processor with metal blade. Return mixtures separately to same pots.

Cook each puréed bean mixture over low heat until hot. Soups should be thin; if not, add a little water. Taste and add salt if necessary.

To serve, ladle about ½ cup black bean soup in warm, shallow soup bowl. Carefully ladle ½ cup white bean soup in center of bowl. Repeat with remaining soups.

Garnish each bowl with a nasturtium flower. Makes 6 to 8 servings.

Cucumber Refrigerator Pickles

4 pounds (1 gallon) cucumbers, sliced
1 quart white vinegar, 5% acid-strength
3 cups sugar
1 cup fresh dill weed, chopped
1 tablespoon pickling spice
1 tablespoon whole black pepper
8 cloves garlic, sliced

Place cucumber slices in clean, 1-gallon glass jar with tight-fitting lid.

Stir together vinegar and remaining ingredients in large bowl until well mixed. (Sugar need not dissolve.)

Pour mixture over cucumbers. Cover with plastic wrap and lid.

Refrigerate 3 days, carefully inverting jar once each day. Keeps up to 3 months in refrigerator. Makes 1 gallon.

Salads and Salad Dressings

An easy way to find out how well you like the flavor of a certain herb is to add just a few leaves to a salad.

A trip to your herb garden can make ordinary salads special. For a quick salad, just snip a few leaves of your favorite herbs, toss them with salad ingredients, add a few slices of sun-ripe tomatoes, top with minced herbs, and drizzle with olive oil and vinegar. Herbs can also be the main ingredients of a salad, as in Watercress and Nectarine Salad.

Watercress and Nectarine Salad

Citrus Dressing (recipe follows)
1 medium head Boston lettuce, torn into bite-size pieces
1 bunch watercress, torn into bite-size pieces
2 nectarines, each cut into 8 wedges

Prepare Citrus Dressing.

Toss together lettuce, watercress, and nectarines in large bowl. Pour dressing over salad; toss to coat well.
Makes about 7 cups, or 6 servings.

Citrus Dressing: Whisk together ½ cup dairy sour cream, 6 tablespoons grapefruit juice, 2 teaspoons sugar, and ¼ teaspoon ground ginger in small bowl.
Cover and refrigerate at least 2 hours to blend flavors.

Tabouli with Bean Sprouts

1 cup bulgar wheat, cracked
2 cups fresh mung bean sprouts
2 medium tomatoes, peeled, seeded, and coarsely chopped
1 medium green pepper, chopped
½ cup carrots, shredded
½ cup fresh parsley, chopped

¼ cup onion, finely chopped
¼ cup lemon juice
¼ cup vegetable oil
1 tablespoon chopped fresh spearmint or 1 teaspoon dried spearmint
½ teaspoon salt
⅛ teaspoon pepper
1 clove garlic, minced

Place cracked wheat in large bowl. Cover with warm water and soak 2 hours. Drain well.

Toss soaked cracked wheat and remaining ingredients together in large bowl until well mixed.

Cover and refrigerate at least 2 hours to blend flavors, stirring occasionally. Makes about 5 cups, or 6 to 8 servings.

Borage and Cucumber in Sour Cream Dressing

3 long cucumbers
Salt
1 cup dairy sour cream or plain yogurt
¼ cup young borage leaves, finely chopped
¼ cup green onions, chopped

2 tablespoons rice vinegar
1 teaspoon sugar
½ teaspoon celery seed
Pepper
Borage flowers or chive blossoms

Wash, score, and thinly slice cucumbers. Salt lightly and let stand in colander 30 minutes to drain.

Rinse cucumber and pat dry with paper towels.

Mix remaining ingredients except flowers in medium bowl. Add salt and pepper to taste.

Cover and refrigerate 1 hour. Garnish with flowers. Makes 6 to 8 servings.

The Windowsill Herb Garden

Tomato, Opal Basil, and Mozzarella Salad

5 tablespoons olive oil
2 tablespoons red wine
   vinegar
2 tablespoons fresh opal
   basil, chopped
1 tablespoon fresh
   parsley, chopped
1 teaspoon lemon juice
1 clove garlic, chopped

Salt
Pepper
Leaf lettuce leaves
4 large tomatoes, cut into
   ¼-inch slices
8 ounces Mozzarella
   cheese, thinly sliced
1 red onion, thinly sliced
Opal basil sprigs

Place first 6 ingredients in blender container or food processor with metal blade. Cover and process until well blended. Season with salt and pepper to taste.

Line large serving dish with lettuce leaves. Arrange alternating slices of tomato and Mozzarella cheese in rows, overlapping slices.

Spoon dressing over salad. Top with onion rings and garnish with opal basil sprigs. Makes 6 servings.

Fresh Herb Vinaigrette

¾ cup vinegar
½ cup olive or vegetable
   oil
3 tablespoons chopped
   fresh herbs (basil,
   chervil, chives, dill,
   marjoram, rose-
   mary, sage, savory,
   tarragon, or thyme)

2 tablespoons white wine
   or sherry
¼ teaspoon salt
¼ teaspoon pepper
1 clove garlic, minced
2 ounces feta or blue
   cheese, crumbled
   (optional)

Combine all ingredients in shaker jar. Cover and shake well. Makes about 1½ cups.

Basic Herbed Salad Dressing

½ cup wine vinegar
½ cup light olive oil
1 to 2 tablespoons lemon
 juice
2 to 3 tablespoons
 chopped fresh herbs
 (equal parts of basil,
 parsley, thyme, and
 oregano; or basil,
savory, and thyme;
 or thyme, chives
 and basil)
½ teaspoon sugar
½ teaspoon Dijon or
 prepared mustard
1 clove garlic, halved
Salad greens

Place all ingredients except garlic and salad greens in blender container. Cover and blend at high speed until smooth.

Let stand 1 hour at room temperature to blend flavors.

Rub salad bowl with cut halves of garlic. Add salad greens and dressing; toss to coat well. Makes about ¾ cup.

Herbed Yogurt Dressing

2 cups plain yogurt
¼ cup mayonnaise or
 salad dressing
¼ cup chopped fresh dill
 weed or 4 teaspoons
 dried dill weed
¼ cup fresh parsley,
 chopped
2 green onions, chopped
1 small clove garlic,
 minced
2 tablespoons lemon
 juice
2 teaspoons sugar

Whisk together all ingredients in small bowl.

Cover and refrigerate at least 12 hours to blend flavors. Keeps up to 2 weeks in refrigerator. Makes 2⅓ cups.

The Windowsill Herb Garden

Decidedly Dill Dressing

⅔ cups vegetable oil
⅓ cup white wine
    vinegar
2 tablespoons chopped
    fresh dill weed or 2
    teaspoons dried dill
    weed

1 teaspoon sugar
½ teaspoon salt
¼ teaspoon pepper
⅛ teaspoon garlic powder

Place all ingredients in jar with tight-fitting lid. Cover and shake until well mixed.

Refrigerate at least 2 hours to blend flavors. Keeps up to 1 month in refrigerator. Makes 1 cup.

Green Goddess Dressing

1 cup mayonnaise or
    salad dressing
¾ cup fresh parsley
    sprigs, lightly
    packed
3 anchovy fillets
2 green onions, cut up
1 small clove garlic,
    quartered

3 tablespoons milk
2 tablespoons lemon
    juice
1 teaspoon dried tarragon
    leaves
½ teaspoon sugar
¼ teaspoon salt
⅛ teaspoon pepper
½ cup dairy sour cream

Place all ingredients except sour cream in blender container. Cover and blend at high speed until smooth, stopping several times to scrape down sides of blender.

Pour into bowl. Fold in sour cream.

Cover and refrigerate at least 12 hours to blend flavors. Keeps up to 2 weeks in refrigerator. Makes ¾ cup.

Creamy Cress Salad Dressing

2 cups watercress, tightly packed
6 green onions, finely chopped
⅔ cup olive or vegetable oil
1 teaspoon pepper
½ teaspoon salt
¼ cup dairy sour cream, or 2 tablespoons dairy sour cream and 2 tablespoons plain yogurt

Place all ingredients except sour cream in food processor bowl with metal blade. Cover and process until well mixed.

Slowly add sour cream while machine is running. Blend thoroughly.

Cover and refrigerate. Makes about 1 cup.

Creamy Cucumber-Dill Dressing

1 cup dairy sour cream
½ cup cucumber, chopped and seeded
2 tablespoons chopped fresh dill weed or 2 teaspoons dried dill weed
1 tablespoon onion, minced
1 tablespoon lemon juice
2 teaspoons sugar
⅛ teaspoon garlic salt

Stir all ingredients together in small bowl until well blended.

Cover and refrigerate at least 12 hours to blend flavors. Keeps up to 2 weeks in refrigerator. Makes 1⅓ cups.

Entrees

Fresh herbs added to meat should complement, not overpower, the flavor of the meat. Choose herbs such as dill, fennel, and lemon thyme to season poultry, pork, and fish. With beef or lamb, you can use stronger herbs such as oregano, rosemary, and marjoram.

Cheesy Chive Blossom Omelet

4 eggs
1 teaspoon water
1 teaspoon fresh parsley, chopped
¼ teaspoon salt
⅛ teaspoon white pepper
1 tablespoon sweet butter

3 young chive blossoms, broken into flowerettes
2 tablespoons Swiss cheese, shredded
Whole chive blossoms

Whisk together eggs, water, parsley, salt, and pepper in small bowl.

Melt butter in 10-inch omelet pan over medium-high heat, until hot and bubbly. Pour in egg mixture, shaking pan.

Stir eggs with fork. Shake and tilt pan until eggs begin to set.

Sprinkle chive flowerettes and cheese down center. Cook until cheese melts slightly.

Fold omelet in half and slip onto plate. Garnish with whole chive blossoms. Makes 2 servings.

Quick Chicken Scallopine

2 whole chicken breasts, halved, boned, and skinned
3 tablespoons butter or margarine
1 tablespoon olive or vegetable oil
¼ cup white wine
¼ cup whipping cream
2 tablespoons coarsely chopped fresh herbs (basil, chervil, chives, dill, marjoram, rosemary, tarragon, or thyme)
⅛ teaspoon black pepper
Fresh herb sprigs

Place each chicken breast half between two pieces of plastic wrap. Pound to ¼-inch thickness with meat mallet.

Heat butter and oil in large skillet over medium-high heat. Add chicken a few pieces at a time; brown quickly on both sides. Cook about 2 minutes, or until no longer pink in center. Place chicken pieces on platter and keep warm.

Scrape up all bits of meat sticking to skillet; stir in wine and bring to a boil. Reduce heat and simmer 2 minutes.

Stir in cream, herbs, and pepper. Cook 1 minute more, until mixture thickens slightly.

Spoon sauce over chicken. Garnish with herb sprigs. Makes 2 to 3 servings.

Thai Chicken with Basil

3 to 4 tablespoons green chiles, finely chopped and seeded
2 tablespoons soy sauce
1 teaspoon sugar
1 teaspoon vinegar
½ cup fresh basil, chopped
1 teaspoon chopped fresh mint or ½ teaspoon dried mint
½ teaspoon cornstarch
3 tablespoons vegetable oil
2 whole chicken breasts (about 1 pound each), boned, skinned, and cut into ¼-inch strips about 2 inches long
2 cloves garlic, minced
1 large onion, halved, then sliced into ¼-inch wedges
Hot cooked rice

Stir together chiles, soy sauce, sugar, vinegar, basil, mint, and cornstarch in small bowl. Set aside.

Heat 2 tablespoons of the oil in wok or large skillet over high heat. Add chicken and garlic. Cook, stirring constantly, until chicken is tender. Remove chicken from pan with slotted spoon; keep warm.

In same wok, heat another tablespoon oil and add onion. Cook, stirring, 2 minutes. Add chile mixture and chicken. Cook, stirring, until sauce thickens.

Serve over rice. Makes 4 to 6 servings.

Grilled Lamb with Mustard Tarragon Marinade

3-pound leg of lamb,
    boned and
    butterflied
2 or 3 cloves garlic,
    thinly slivered
6 fresh tarragon sprigs or
    2 teaspoons dried
    tarragon

2 tablespoons medium-
    dry sherry
¼ cup whole-grain
    mustard
2 tablespoons olive oil
½ teaspoon black
    peppercorns,
    cracked

Make incisions in lamb about 1 inch apart. Insert 1 garlic sliver and 1 tarragon leaf into each incision.

Stem and mince remaining tarragon, or soak dried tarragon in sherry.

Mix tarragon, sherry, mustard, oil, and pepper in small bowl. Rub mixture all over lamb.

Cover and refrigerate overnight.

Prepare a medium-hot charcoal fire and remove lamb from refrigerator about 1 hour before grilling.

Grill lamb 5 inches above coals, turning 4 or 5 times. Check for doneness after 12 minutes for rare lamb, or continue cooking until desired doneness is obtained.

Let lamb rest at least 5 minutes before carving.

To serve, slice lamb diagonally across the grain of the meat into ⅜-inch slices. Makes 6 to 8 servings.

Butterflied Basil Shrimp

1 pound large shrimp,
  shelled, deveined,
  tails left on
1/3 to 1/2 cup olive oil
1 large clove garlic,
  minced
1/2 cup fresh basil, packed
  and finely chopped

3 tablespoons dry
  vermouth
3 tablespoons lemon
  juice
Salt
Pepper
Lemon slices
Basil leaves ·
Boston lettuce leaves

Butterfly shrimp by cutting along inner curve, almost but not all the way through.

Heat oil in large skillet over medium heat. Add garlic, basil, vermouth, and lemon juice. Add shrimp and cook, stirring constantly, 2 to 4 minutes, or until shrimp are pink and tender.

Remove from heat. Sprinkle with salt and pepper to taste. Spoon into bowl.

Cover and refrigerate 1 to 2 hours to blend flavors. Return shrimp mixture to room temperature.

To serve as an appetizer, skewer shrimp, lemon slices, and basil leaves on decorative wooden picks. Makes about 20.

To serve as a salad, line 4 plates with Boston lettuce leaves; arrange shrimp with sauce on top. Garnish with lemon slices and basil leaves. Makes 4 servings.

Linguini with Fresh Parsley Clam Sauce

2 cans (6½ ounces each)
  chopped clams
2 to 3 green onions,
  finely chopped
2 small cloves garlic,
  minced
1 to 2 tablespoons olive
  oil
1 cup half-and-half or
  whole milk
1 cup fresh parsley,
  chopped

1 cup Parmesan cheese,
  grated
½ pound linguini,
  cooked and drained
Salt
Pepper
1 large tomato, seeded
  and coarsely
  chopped
1 tablespoon lemon juice

Drain clams; reserve liquid. Set both aside.

Cook onions and garlic until tender in oil over medium heat in deep, 12-inch skillet. Add reserved clam juice and half-and-half.

Simmer about 8 to 10 minutes, until reduced and thickened. Stir in clams and parsley; simmer 5 minutes more.

Remove from heat. Add cheese and cooked linguini. Toss to coat well. Season with salt and pepper to taste.

Spoon onto serving platter. Sprinkle with chopped tomato and lemon juice. Makes 4 to 6 servings.

Fillet of Sole with Crab

1 cup cooked crab meat (do not use frozen crab)
2 tablespoons *créme fraiche*
White pepper
Pinch cayenne pepper
4 fillets (about 1 pound) sole
1 tablespoon unsalted butter

1 medium shallot, minced
½ cup dry white wine
1 tablespoon tarragon, minced
Salt
½ cup heavy or whipping cream

Gently mix crab meat, *créme fraiche*, a pinch of white pepper, and cayenne pepper in small bowl.

Divide mixture into fourths. Roll each sole fillet with one fourth crab mixture. Tie with kitchen string or secure with wooden picks.

Cook shallot in butter until tender in small skillet over medium heat. Stir in wine, tarragon, salt, and a pinch of white pepper. Simmer 5 minutes.

continued on next page

Add filled fillets and poach gently about 5 minutes, carefully turning them once.

Remove cooked fillets with slotted spoon to warm platter; keep warm.

Increase heat under sauce and reduce to ⅓ cup. Add cream. Heat, but do not boil. Spoon sauce into warm serving dish.

Remove strings or picks from fillets and place fillets over sauce. Serve immediately. Makes 4 servings.

Vegetables and Sauces

Many vegetables are savored for their characteristic flavors. For vegetables with strong flavors, use mild-flavored herbs. For example, you can use snips of lemon balm to enhance broccoli, or chopped lovage to season cauliflower. Mild-flavored vegetables, such as potatoes, carrots, and green beans, can be seasoned with stronger herbs such as tarragon, oregano and basil. With tomatoes, you can use just about any herb you like.

Sauces are great carriers for herbs. Add your favorite mix of herbs to White Sauce Supreme. Try the basil- and garlic-flavored Pesto as a topping for cooked pasta. Cilantro is the main ingredient of Salsa, which is a great dip for corn chips and topping for barbecued chicken.

Roasted Potatoes with Garlic and Herbs

3 tablespoons olive oil
½ to 1 head garlic, separated into cloves and peeled
12 small or 6 medium potatoes, cut into

½-inch slices and patted dry
4 or 5 sprigs (each 4 to 6 inches) basil, rosemary, or thyme

Toss oil and garlic in 13×9×2-inch baking dish. Add potato slices and toss again to coat well.

Arrange potato slices in single layer; place herb sprigs on top.

Cover and bake in 400° F oven 20 minutes. Uncover and bake 15 to 20 minutes longer, or until potatoes are tender and begin to brown.

Carefully remove herb sprigs and discard. Serve potatoes immediately. Makes 4 to 6 servings.

Golden Brown Chive Roast Potatoes

6 large baking potatoes
¼ cup butter, melted
½ teaspoon salt
½ cup cheese, shredded
   or grated
¼ cup fresh chives,
   chopped
3 tablespoons dried
   bread crumbs

Cut a thin slice from long side of each potato so they do not roll. With sharp knife, cut vertical slits from top of each potato to within ⅛ inch of bottom. Be careful not to cut through potato.

Dip cut potatoes in melted butter and sprinkle with salt. Place on foil-covered baking sheet.

Bake in 350° F oven 1½ hours, basting with remaining butter. Potatoes will turn a crisp, golden brown and slits will open like a fan as they bake.

Combine cheese, chives, and bread crumbs in small bowl during last 15 minutes of baking. Stuff mixture into slits in potatoes.

Return potatoes to oven. Bake 1 to 2 minutes more, until cheese melts. Serve immediately. Makes 6 servings.

Butternut Purée with Thyme

1 (1½-pound) butternut
   squash, halved
   lengthwise and
   seeded
2 to 3 tablespoons
   unsalted butter
1 tablespoon honey
2 teaspoons fresh thyme,
   finely chopped
Salt
White pepper

Place squash halves, cut-side down, on baking sheet. Cover with foil. Bake in 375° F oven 1 hour, or until squash is fork-tender.

Remove from oven; set aside until cool enough to handle.

Scoop out meat and purée through food mill into 2-quart greased baking dish. Stir in butter, honey, and thyme. Taste and season with salt and pepper.

Bake in 400° F oven 20 to 25 minutes, or until hot. Makes 6 servings.

Haricots Verts Parisian Style

3 cups *haricots verts*,
    Chinese long beans,
    or green beans,
    stringed and cut
    into 2-inch pieces
3 tablespoons butter or
    margarine
1 tablespoon lemon or
    lime juice

1 tablespoon fresh chervil
    or chives, chopped
1 tablespoon fresh basil,
    savory, sage, or
    tarragon, chopped
1½ teaspoons lemon or
    lime peel, shredded
2 tablespoons pimiento
    slices

Steam beans in medium saucepan over boiling water about 8 minutes, or until nearly tender.

Meanwhile, melt butter in small saucepan over low heat. Stir in lemon juice, herbs, and lemon peel until blended. Remove from heat.

Spoon beans onto plate. Pour butter sauce over beans and add pimiento. Toss to coat well. Makes 4 servings.

(This butter sauce also can be used over any cooked vegetable, fish, or poultry.)

Spiced Mushrooms

⅓ cup olive oil
1½ pounds medium
    button mushrooms,
    stemmed
1 teaspoon fenugreek
    seed

6 black peppercorns
1 teaspoon pickling spice
1 cup dry white wine
¼ cup red wine vinegar
2 large bay leaves
1 teaspoon salt

Heat oil in large skillet over medium heat. Add mushrooms and sauté 3 minutes, shaking pan to coat mushrooms.

Tie fenugreek seed, peppercorns, and pickling spice in cheesecloth to make spice bag.

Add spice bag, wine, vinegar, bay leaves, and salt to mushrooms. Simmer 10 minutes. Remove from heat. Pour mixture in glass dish.

Cover and refrigerate at least 4 hours. Let stand at room temperature 1 hour before serving. Remove spice bag and bay leaves. Makes 6 to 8 servings.

Gorgonzola and Fresh Thyme Sauce for Pasta

1½ cups heavy or
    whipping cream
6 ounces aged
    Gorgonzola cheese,
    crumbled
1 teaspoon fresh thyme
    or ½ teaspoon dried
    thyme
2 to 3 generous grates
    nutmeg or ⅛
    teaspoon ground
    nutmeg
Salt
White pepper
Hot cooked pasta

Stir together cream, cheese, thyme, and nutmeg in large skillet.

Cook gently over medium heat until mixture reduces by one-fourth. Add salt and pepper to taste.

Toss with pasta to coat well. Serve with extra nutmeg if desired. Makes 2 servings.

White Sauce Supreme

2 tablespoons butter or
    margarine
2 tablespoons flour
1¼ cups milk
¼ cup coarsely chopped
    fresh herbs (basil,
    dill, chervil, chives,
    marjoram, oregano,
rosemary, tarragon,
    or thyme)
⅛ teaspoon pepper
1 (3-ounce) package
    cream cheese,
    softened and cut up
3 tablespoons white wine

Melt butter in 2-quart saucepan over medium heat. Whisk in flour until smooth and well blended. Stir in milk, then herbs and pepper. Cook, stirring constantly, until mixture boils and thickens.

Add cream cheese a few cubes at a time, until melted. Stir in wine and heat 1 minute more.

Serve over vegetables, poultry, or seafood, or mix with cooked rice. Makes 1¾ cups.

Homemade Dilled Mustard

1 cup dry mustard
1 cup cider vinegar
¾ cup sugar
¼ cup water

2 tablespoons fresh dill
   weed, chopped
2 teaspoons salt
2 eggs, slightly beaten

Mix all ingredients except eggs in small bowl. Cover and let stand 4 to 6 hours.

Pour mustard mixture into top of double boiler. Place double boiler top over hot, but not boiling, water. Add eggs. Cook, stirring constantly, about 10 minutes, until mixture thickens.

Pour into small ½-cup containers. Cover and refrigerate.

Keep refrigerated. Makes about 2 cups.

Bay Mustard Sauce

2 tablespoons unsalted
   butter
2 tablespoons flour
1 cup half-and-half
1 bay leaf

1 cup beef stock or broth
3 tablespoons Dijon
   mustard
Salt

Melt butter in heavy 1-quart saucepan over medium heat. Stir in flour until smooth.

Scald half-and-half with bay leaf in another saucepan.

Gradually stir beef stock and hot half-and-half into flour mixture until smooth. Stir in mustard. Cook, stirring constantly, until sauce boils and thickens.

Remove bay leaf. Taste and season with salt. Makes about 2 cups.

Béarnaise Sauce

¼ cup white wine
2 tablespoons tarragon
    vinegar
1 tablespoon onion,
    finely chopped
1 teaspoon fresh parsley,
    chopped

1 teaspoon chopped fresh
    tarragon or ¼ tea-
    spoon dried tarragon
Dash pepper
3 egg yolks
¾ cup butter or margarine,
    cut into tablespoons

Cook first 6 ingredients in 1-quart saucepan over medium-high heat about 3 minutes, until mixture is reduced by half. Remove from heat. Strain, reserving wine mixture.

Whisk egg yolks in double boiler top. Rapidly beat in wine mixture.

Place double boiler top over hot, but not boiling, water. Cook, stirring constantly, until egg yolk mixture thickens slightly. Beat in butter, 1 tablespoon at time, until melted. Continue cooking, stirring constantly, until sauce is light and fluffy.

Serve immediately. Makes 1 cup.

Pesto

2 cups fresh basil leaves,
    packed
¾ cup olive or vegetable
    oil
½ cup Parmesan cheese,
    grated

½ cup fresh parsley
    sprigs, lightly packed
¼ cup pine nuts or
    walnuts
2 cloves garlic, quartered

Place all ingredients in food processor with metal blade and cover. Process until mixture is finely chopped, but not mushy.

Spoon into container. Coat thinly with oil to prevent darkening.

Cover and refrigerate 2 hours to blend flavors. Keeps up to 2 weeks in refrigerator. Makes 1¼ cups.

To freeze, line large baking sheet with plastic wrap. Drop Pesto by tablespoonfuls onto plastic wrap. Cover with another sheet of plastic wrap.

Freeze about 2 hours, until firm.

Remove pesto cubes from baking sheet and place in freezer container. Cover and store in freezer up to 1 year.

continued on next page

Pesto Butter: Mix ½ cup softened butter or margarine in small bowl at high speed until light and fluffy. Beat in ¼ cup Pesto until well blended.
Makes ⅔ cup.

Aioli Sauce

1 slice firm bread, crust removed	¼ teaspoon salt
3 tablespoons milk	1½ cups olive oil
1 to 3 cloves garlic, quartered	3 tablespoons lemon juice
2 egg yolks	Hot water

Soak bread in milk in small bowl 5 minutes. Squeeze out milk.

Place bread and garlic in blender container or food processor with metal blade. Cover and blend at high speed until mixture forms a rough paste.

Add egg yolks and salt. Blend until well mixed.

With blender running at high speed, gradually pour oil in steady stream through center of cover until mixture is thick. (Mixture will look like mayonnaise.) Add lemon juice, 1 tablespoon at a time. Blend in about 3 tablespoons hot water, enough to make a thick sauce. Pour sauce into bowl.

Cover and refrigerate 2 hours to blend flavors. Keeps up to 2 weeks in refrigerator. Makes 2 cups.

Mayonnaise *Vert*

1 large egg	½ cup watercress leaves and stems
4½ teaspoons lemon or lime juice	2 tablespoons fresh basil, coarsely chopped
1 teaspoon Dijon mustard	2 tablespoons coarsely chopped fresh dill, tarragon, or thyme
¼ teaspoon salt	
⅛ teaspoon pepper	
3 tablespoons olive oil	1 tablespoon fresh chives, chopped
1¼ cups vegetable oil	

Place first 6 ingredients in blender container. Cover and blend at high speed until smooth.

With blender running, gradually pour vegetable oil in a thin stream until well blended. Mixture will thicken as more oil is added.

Stop blender. Add watercress, basil, dill, and chives. Cover and blend until smooth. Makes about 1⅔ cups.

Oregano Hot Sauce

4 large jalapeño peppers, seeded and minced
2 pounds ripe tomatoes, peeled, seeded, and finely diced, or 1 can (1 pound) plum tomatoes, finely diced

1 small white onion, minced
1 tablespoon fresh oregano leaves, minced
Salt
Pepper

Stir together peppers, tomatoes, onion, and oregano in medium bowl. Taste and season with salt and pepper.

Let stand 1 hour to blend flavors. Makes 2 cups.

Salsa Fresca

9 green onions, white part only, coarsely chopped
4 small tomatoes, finely chopped
3 or 4 mild green chiles, roasted, peeled, seeded, and finely chopped
2 or 3 fresh serrano or jalapeño peppers,

seeded and finely chopped
1 clove garlic, finely chopped
1 tablespoon fresh cilantro, chopped
1 teaspoon red wine vinegar
½ teaspoon salt
⅛ teaspoon pepper
⅛ teaspoon sugar

Stir together all ingredients in medium bowl.

Serve immediately, or cover and refrigerate up to 2 days.

If salsa gets watery, pour off excess liquid before serving. Makes 3 to 4 cups.

Salsa de Tomatillos

2 pounds fresh tomatillos
¼ cup water
½ teaspoon salt
¼ cup green onions, cut
    in 1-inch pieces
¼ cup cilantro leaves

3 to 4 fresh jalapeño
    peppers, halved,
    cored, and seeded
1 teaspoon lemon juice
1 teaspoon garlic, minced
½ teaspoon sugar

Peel husks from tomatillos. Wash off sticky residue in cold water.

Bring water and salt to a boil in medium saucepan over medium heat. Add tomatillos.

Cover and cook about 5 minutes, or until softened.

Remove from heat and place in food processor bowl with metal blade. Add remaining ingredients. Cover and process into a thick purée.

Cover and refrigerate up to 3 days. Makes 3 to 4 cups.

Lemon Basil Marinade for Grilled Fish or Chicken

½ cup fresh lemon basil,
    finely chopped
⅓ cup lemon juice
2 tablespoons dry white
    wine
2 teaspoons Dijon
    mustard

½ teaspoon salt
¼ teaspoon pepper
3 green onions, thinly
    sliced
1 cup olive oil

Stir together all ingredients except oil in small bowl. Gradually whisk in oil until mixture is smooth and blended.

Marinate fish or chicken at least 3 hours or overnight before grilling. Makes 1½ cups.

Sour Cream-Dill Topping

1 cup dairy sour cream
2 tablespoons chopped
   fresh dill weed or

2 teaspoons dried dill
   weed

Stir together sour cream and dill weed in small bowl. Cover and refrigerate at least 2 hours to blend flavors. Keeps up to 2 weeks in refrigerator. Makes 1 cup.

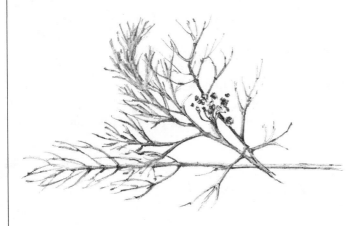

Butters and Seasoning Blends

An interesting way to add the taste of herbs to your food is to make herb butters. These flavor-packed butters are easy to make and can be used on vegetables, meats, or as cracker spreads. Once you try the recipe for Fresh Herb Butter, you'll want to experiment with your own spreads.

Herbs are also great salt substitutes. After trying any of the following dried herb blends, you may decide to replace the salt in your salt shaker with herbs.

One of the most important and delicious fresh herb blends is *Fines Herbes*, widely used as seasoning in French cuisine. Although the mixture can vary, *Fines Herbes* generally consists of equal parts of parsley, tarragon, chives, and chervil, finely chopped or minced together. You can use it to season eggs, soups, fish, stews, and meats.

Fresh Herb Butter

½ cup butter or
   margarine, softened
3 tablespoons fresh
   herbs, minced

2 teaspoons lemon juice
1 teaspoon Dijon mustard

Place all ingredients in blender or food processor with metal blade. Cover and process until smooth.

Cover and refrigerate until ready to use. Makes about ½ cup.

Fresh Herb Butter Log: Prepare Fresh Herb Butter as directed.

Place herb butter on a square of plastic wrap and shape into a log 6 inches long. Wrap tightly and refrigerate until firm.

Place ⅓ cup chopped fresh parsley on another sheet of plastic wrap. Roll butter log in parsley to coat. Wrap and refrigerate.

Let stand at room temperature about 15 minutes before serving. Cut into slices. Makes 24 (¼-inch-thick) slices.

Mixed Herb Butter

¼ cup butter or
   margarine
2 teaspoons onion,
   chopped
2 teaspoons chopped
   fresh basil or ½
   teaspoon dried basil

2 teaspoons chopped
   fresh dill weed or ½
   teaspoon dried dill
   weed
¼ teaspoon dried
   tarragon leaves,
   crushed
⅛ teaspoon salt

Beat butter in small bowl with mixer at high speed until light and fluffy. Beat in onion and remaining ingredients until well blended.

Cover and refrigerate at least 2 hours to blend flavors. Keeps up to 2 weeks in refrigerator. Makes ¼ cup.

The Windowsill Herb Garden

Sorrel and Shallot Butter

½ cup unsalted butter, softened
½ cup fresh sorrel leaves, finely chopped

3 tablespoons shallots, chopped
1 clove garlic, chopped
3 drops Tabasco sauce
Salt

Stir together first 5 ingredients in small bowl. Add salt to taste.

Serve over cooked vegetables, broiled steak, or chicken. Makes about ¾ cup.

Lemon-Parsley Butter

¼ cup butter or margarine, softened
1 tablespoon fresh parsley, chopped

1 teaspoon lemon juice
⅛ teaspoon salt
⅛ teaspoon pepper

Beat butter in small bowl with mixer at high speed until light and fluffy. Beat in parsley, lemon juice, salt, and pepper until well blended.

Cover and refrigerate at least 2 hours to blend flavors. Keeps up to 2 weeks in refrigerator. Makes ¼ cup.

Savory Peach Butter

6 pounds ripe peaches, peeled, pitted, and each cut into 8 slices

1⅓ cups light honey

2 tablespoons lemon juice

8 (6-inch-long) summer savory sprigs

5 (3-inch-long) summer savory sprigs

Place peach slices in stainless steel saucepot. Bring to a boil over low heat. Cover and simmer 1 hour, stirring frequently.

Remove from heat. Let stand 30 minutes, stirring occasionally.

Purée peach mixture in food processor with metal blade.

Return peach mixture to pan. Stir in honey, lemon juice, and 6-inch summer savory sprigs. Cook over low heat, stirring frequently, until mixture is medium-thick. Butter thickens as it cools.

Remove savory sprigs. Ladle butter into 5 hot, sterilized, half-pint jars, leaving ½-inch space at top.

Add a 3-inch savory sprig to each jar. Wipe rims of jars with damp cloth. Cover with lids according to jar manufacturer's directions.

Process in boiling water bath 10 minutes once water in canner boils. Remove jars.

Cool on racks 12 to 24 hours. Check jars for airtight seal. Makes 5 half-pints.

Dill Butter

¼ cup butter or margarine, softened

1 tablespoon onion, finely chopped

2 teaspoons chopped fresh dill weed or ½ teaspoon dried dill weed

⅛ teaspoon salt

Beat butter in small bowl with mixer at high speed until light and fluffy. Beat in onion, dill, and salt until well blended.

Cover and refrigerate at least 2 hours to blend flavors. Keeps up to 2 weeks in refrigerator. Makes ¼ cup.

The Windowsill Herb Garden

Bouquet Garni

1 4-inch square of
    cheesecloth
2 fresh or dried bay
    leaves
1 large clove garlic
1 wedge lemon

1 sprig fresh parsley
2 to 3 sprigs or leaves
    fresh basil, lemon
    grass, sage, savory,
    tarragon, or thyme

Lay cheesecloth flat. Place all ingredients in center.
Bring corners of cheesecloth together and tie with
kitchen string into a bundle.

Add *Bouquet Garni* when adding liquids to soup,
stew, or roast recipes. Simmer along with your recipe at
least 1 hour to infuse full flavor.

Remove and discard just before serving. Makes 1
bouquet.

Herbed Flour

2 cups all-purpose flour
2 tablespoons crushed
    dried herbs (basil,

dill, marjoram, parsley,
    savory, or thyme)
½ teaspoon pepper

Combine all ingredients in glass jar.

Keep in jar. Use to dust chicken or fish, or in place
of flour in biscuit, pizza crust, or muffin recipes.

Store in refrigerator. Makes 2 cups.

Low-Sodium French Seasoning Blend

1 tablespoon marjoram
    leaves
2 teaspoons thyme leaves
2 teaspoons instant
    minced onion

1 teaspoon instant
    minced garlic
½ teaspoon black
    pepper, coarsely
    ground

Combine all ingredients in small bowl.
Store in covered jar. Makes ¼ cup.

Herb Blend

2 tablespoons dried dill weed, crushed
2 tablespoons onion powder
1 teaspoon oregano leaves, crushed

1 teaspoon celery seed
¼ teaspoon lemon peel, dried and grated
$\frac{1}{16}$ teaspoon ground black pepper

Combine all ingredients in small bowl. Store in covered jar. Makes ⅓ cup.

Herb Seasoning Blend

1 tablespoon dried parsley, crushed
1 tablespoon paprika
1 tablespoon dried dill weed, crushed

1 tablespoon basil leaves, crushed
½ teaspoon onion powder

Combine all ingredients in small bowl. Store in covered jar. Makes ¼ cup.

Herbal Salt Substitute

2 tablespoons dried dill weed
2 tablespoons sesame seed, toasted
2 tablespoons onion powder or finely ground onion flakes
1 teaspoon dried oregano leaves, crushed

1 teaspoon celery seed
½ teaspoon garlic powder
½ teaspoon paprika
¼ teaspoon lemon peel, dried and grated
Pinch pepper

Combine all ingredients in small bowl. Pour into shaker with large holes.

Store in cool, dark place. Sprinkle over vegetables, salad, or bread. Makes about ⅓ cup.

The Windowsill Herb Garden

Blackened Seasoning Blend

1 tablespoon paprika
2 teaspoons dried thyme
    leaves, crushed
1 teaspoon onion powder
1 teaspoon garlic powder

1 teaspoon salt
1 teaspoon sugar
1 teaspoon black pepper
½ teaspoon cayenne
    pepper

Combine all ingredients in small bowl.
Store in a covered jar. Makes 3 tablespoons.

Vinegars

A wonderful way to add flavor to sauces, dressings, and salads is to make them with herb-flavor vinegars. The procedure is simple, and you'll want to try your hand at making your own combinations.

You can use any kind of vinegar: distilled, cider, wine, or rice wine. Remember that the stronger the flavor of the vinegar, the more it will overpower the herbs. For red wine or cider vinegar, try using stronger herbs such as oregano or rosemary.

For each quart of vinegar, put about a cup of herbs in a 1-quart glass jar.

Heat 3½ cups of vinegar until hot, but do not boil. Pour into jar with herbs and cool. Cover with a nonmetal lid.

Let the vinegar stand in a cool, dark place up to a year. Taste before using—if the herb flavor is too strong, dilute by adding more vinegar.

To make more-than-just-herb vinegar, you can add garlic cloves, shallots, or chiles along with the herbs.

Decorative bottles of herb vinegar make welcome holiday presents if put up in fall.

Scented Basil Vinegar

Pack large one-gallon plastic or glass jar half full with rinsed and air-dried leaves, stems, and flowers of anise basil, cinnamon basil, opal basil, or lemon basil.

Fill jar with distilled white vinegar that has been heated almost to a boil. Cover with plastic wrap and lid.

Allow to stand in cool place a month or two to blend flavors.

Strain vinegar through cheesecloth into small, decorative jars or clean wine bottles. Seal with corks or nonmetal tops.

Anise basil and cinnamon basil vinegars are a lovely soft pink, opal basil vinegar is a deep, rich garnet, and lemon basil vinegar is champagne-colored.

Chive Blossom Vinegar

Fill a clean glass or plastic jar halfway with mature chive blossoms whose color has not faded. Fill jar to the top with distilled white vinegar. Make sure all blossoms are covered. Cover with nonmetal lid and set in sun. Blossoms transfer their color and flavor to the vinegar in about 2 to 3 weeks.

Strain through cheesecloth. Taste and dilute with vinegar if chive flavor is too strong.

Decant into attractive glass jars or bottles and seal with corks or nonmetal tops.

The Windowsill Herb Garden

Baked Goods and Desserts

You can easily turn plain biscuits or rolls into something extra special just by adding a few tablespoons of chopped fresh dill, fennel, or basil to the dough before baking.

Herb-flavored desserts are not common. But sample the creamy custard with just a hint of bay or the frosty chervil-flavored sorbet and you may start experimenting with your favorite dessert recipes.

Herbed Bread Sticks

1 small loaf white bread, crust removed, very thinly sliced
¼ teaspoon salt
⅛ teaspoon pepper
1 large clove garlic, chopped
½ cup butter or margarine, softened
¼ cup Parmesan cheese, grated
2 tablespoons fresh parsley, chopped
2 tablespoons fresh chives, chopped
1 tablespoon chopped fresh savory or marjoram, or 1 teaspoon dried
Butter or margarine, melted

Roll each bread slice flat with rolling pin. Set aside.

Mash salt, pepper, and garlic with back of spoon in small bowl. Stir in butter, cheese, and herbs.

Spread one side of each bread slice with herb mixture. Roll up each bread slice jelly-roll fashion and secure with wooden picks.

Place, seam-side down, on baking sheet. Brush lightly with melted butter.

Bake in 350° F oven 12 to 15 minutes, or until lightly brown. Turn sticks several times during baking.

Serve immediately. Makes about 20 sticks.

Marjoram Corn Bread

1½ cups cornmeal, preferably stone-ground
1½ cups whole-wheat flour
1 teaspoon baking powder
1 teaspoon baking soda
¾ teaspoon salt
½ cup wheat germ

2 tablespoons minced fresh marjoram, or 1½ teaspoons crumbled dried marjoram
2 cups milk
¼ cup vegetable oil or melted butter
2 eggs

Sift together first 5 ingredients into large bowl. Stir in wheat germ and marjoram until mixed.

Whisk milk, oil and eggs 1 minute in small bowl. Add to dry ingredients and blend well. Pour batter into buttered, 12-inch pie plate.

Bake in 350° F oven 30 minutes, or until cake tester inserted in center comes out clean.

Let corn bread cool in plate on rack 10 minutes before cutting. Makes 8 servings.

Honeydew Chervil Sorbet

⅓ cup sugar
1 cup boiling water
1 large honeydew melon

¼ cup fresh chervil, lightly packed
1 cup sweet champagne
10 small borage blossoms

Dissolve sugar in water in small bowl. Cool.

Remove seeds from melon and scoop out 3½ cups pulp. Process in batches with syrup and chervil in food processor with metal blade. Pour purée into oblong metal baking pan.

Freeze 1 hour.

Break up frozen melon mixture with spoon. Process until smooth. Freeze again. Repeat one more time, adding champagne before freezing.

About 10 minutes before serving, break up melon mixture again and process until smooth. Spoon into chilled serving glasses and return to freezer 5 minutes.

Garnish with borage blossoms. Makes 8 to 10 servings.

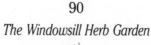

Bay Rum Custard

1½ cups milk
1 cup half-and-half
2 large bay leaves,
    preferably fresh

4 egg yolks
¼ cup honey
Large pinch of salt
2 tablespoons dark rum

Scald milk and half-and-half with bay leaves in 2-quart saucepan over medium heat. Remove from heat and cool 10 minutes.

Remove bay leaves. Whisk in yolks, honey, salt, and rum.

Pour custard into 6 lightly buttered custard cups or 1-quart soufflé dish. Place cups or dish in pan of very hot water. Bake in 350° F oven, 25 to 30 minutes for cups or 45 to 50 minutes for soufflé dish, until set.

Remove from hot water and cool to room temperature.

Refrigerate custard at least 3 hours or overnight.

Let stand at room temperature 1 hour before serving. Makes 6 servings.

Teas

Probably the most familiar use of herbs is in herbal teas. These no-caffeine drinks are increasingly popular.

To make a pot of herbal tea, start with fresh cold water and bring it to a boil.

The next step is to add the herbs. As a guide, use two tablespoons of fresh herbs or one tablespoon of dried herbs for every cup of water. Don't forget to add an extra tablespoon "for the pot." Place herbs in a warmed china, pottery, or other nonmetal teapot. Pour in the boiling water.

Let the tea steep about 5 minutes. Keep the teapot covered to retain heat.

Steeping times vary, so taste the tea several times. When the tea reaches the desired flavor, strain out the herbs. Serve plain or with lemon, honey, brown sugar, or fresh herb sprigs.

Here are a few suggestions for herbal tea combinations to get you started:

- Peppermint and a slice of fresh or pinch of ground ginger
- Spearmint, lemon verbena, sorrel, and lemon thyme
- Marjoram, fennel, and lemon verbena
- Savory, sorrel, and applemint
- Borage and lemon verbena
- Sorrel, rosemary, and thyme

Mulled Rosemary Wine and Black Tea

1 bottle claret wine	1 (3-inch) cinnamon stick
1 quart black tea	6 whole cloves
⅓ cup sugar	2 (3-inch) fresh rosemary
¼ cup mild honey	sprigs
2 oranges, thinly sliced	
and seeded	

Pour wine and tea into 3-quart saucepan. Stir in sugar and remaining ingredients.

Heat over low heat, stirring occasionally. Do not boil. Taste and add additional sugar if desired.

Strain and serve warm. Makes about 2 quarts.

Liqueurs

Herbs are basic ingredients of many liqueurs. Mint flavors creme de menthe, and anise flavors anisette.

To make your own herb liqueurs, simply place some herbs in brandy and let them sit in a cool place for a few days. Taste—if the flavor is strong enough, strain out the herbs. If not, let the brandy sit a few more days. Some herbs to try are mint, lemon balm, marjoram, or fennel.

Simple syrup can be added to the brandy to bring up the flavor. You can make simple syrup by adding a cup of sugar to a half cup of water in a small saucepan. Bring the sugar and water to a boil over medium heat about 5 minutes, or until slightly thickened. Makes about 1 cup of simple syrup.

Naturally Good Recipes

Index

The Windowsill Herb Garden

The Windowsill Herb Garden